"Millions of viewers fell in love with Thom Bierdz on The Young and the Restless unaware that his real life was more dramatic than any soap opera. This book proves he is not just another pretty face - but an artist of substance, power and talent."

— Daniel R. Coleridge, TVGUIDE.COM

"An epic, raw and overwhelming story of tragedy, chaos, humanity, and ultimately compassion. A rare book that dives, unapologetically and uncensored, into the workings of an American family torn apart by matricide and mental illness. Highly recommended!"

— Jeffrey Keen, USABOOKNEWS.COM

"Shakespearean in its tragic underpinnings, FORGIVING TROY fearlessly tackles a litany of societal ills that ostensibly seem insurmountable, yet the book reverberates with the clear ring of redemption. Author - artist - activist Thom Bierdz has dysfunction running through his veins, but just like a junkie in the process of hardcore rehabilitation, he wages a war against his demons."

— Michael Kearns, IN MAGAZINE

Samples of readers' emails received daily

"…your book is stunning…I've been consumed by it all week, either reading it or thinking about it constantly – you have not helped my chronic insomnia any this week. I like to think I'm fairly articulate, especially since I write for a living…but I'm at a loss for words. Your honesty is so raw, your personal journey so haunting, I'm in a mixed state of being pained, empathetic, overwhelmed, exhilarated and incredibly inspired…"

"I have never, ever read such a moving, brutally honest and well written autobiography…I finished reading it last night and said WOW. I really could not believe how one person can go through so much and still be sane…it really is life changing mate. I really believe the book can show people that anything is possible."

"I felt like I was intruding into your soul. Honest, I thought…I shouldn't be here. This is private."

"Your own personal life force literally flows off the pages…"

"Have you ever read any of the books by Richard Bach by any chance? *Jonathon Livingston Seagull*? *Illusions*? Been pondering ad nauseum the last time I was affected quite this way by another book and it suddenly dawned on me…"

"…you may well have written the most self-analytical biography since Brian Wilson's book *Wouldn't It Be Nice*…Congratulations Thom, you're not just another Hollywood bimbo…"

Forgiving
TROY

A True Story of Murder,
Mental Illness, and Recovery

Thom Bierdz

ISBN 978-1-61539-485-2

Paintings reproduced in book with permission from Thom Bierdz.
Front cover left photo by: Gregg Edelman (www.exposedgallery.com)
Front cover right photo by: Marina Rice Bader (www.marinaricebader.com)
Back cover top photo by: Barry King (www.barryking.com)
Back cover bottom photo: Steve Callahan (www.stevecallahan.com)
Book design by: Rosamond Grupp (BookStudio@comcast.net)

Printed in the United States of America

To Mothers

our source of unconditional love

Acknowledgments

This book would not have been possible without the love, support, and kindness of my dad, sister, aunts, cousins, and all the members of my immediate family.

For sharing my life and work, thank you to Joe Argazzi, Doug Bisson, Steve Callahan, Gary Erxleben, Gary Scheuerman, and Steve Williams.

Thanks especially to my editor, Wil Perdue, for displaying his devotion, talent, and integrity by challenging my every sentence to keep this book honest.

And for embracing my story, thank you: Jeffrey Keen, Bill Granger, Alonsay Salon, Marc Alexander, Jamie Anderson, Bradley Bessey, Dr. Tom Bierdz, Jeffrey Blyseth, Pam Brealey, Elise Bromberg, Minda Burr, Becky Cannady, Phil Cannizarro, Robert Cichocki, Wayne Chester, Dennis Christesen, Joe Clapsaddle, Daniel Coleridge, Luis Contreres, Jilly Cook, Lamar Damon, Donalee Darby, Bruce Dent, Kate Diamond, Carol Doyle, Eddie Dyer, Tom Ellis, Ken Faulkner, Robert Gant, Larry Garcia, Stephen Gatta, The Gourmet Grape, Cathy Griffin, Ron Grove, Heidi Gilles, Kevin Haberl, Bill Harris, Emily Heckman, Warren Hohmann, Jennifer Howell, Jon Imparato, Andrew Isen, Nancy Jones, Sarah Kendell, Andrienne Kessler, Barry King, Janet Leong, Jacques Kaplan, Randy Allen Larsen, Neal LaVine, Jean Leigh, Patti Lesser, Kevin McDonald, Valerie McFadden, Colleen McGrann, Gina Meyers, Danne Montague King, Carl Moellenberg, Steve Moore, Bart Mruz, Breanne Munroe, Mark Nagel, Brian Niemark, Dr. Michael Olson, Marcel Pariseau, Mark Peterson, Marina Rice Bader, Tony Rizzo, Nick Salamone, Bob Scarano, Ron Scott, Shig, Amy Shomer, Devin Sidell, Robin Siegel, *Soap Opera Digest,* Doug St. Clair, Anne Stockwell, Rebecca Street, *True Crime Magazine,* Lucien Truscott, Robert Waldron, Brian Waldvogel, David Wareham, Jim Warren, Tony Westbrook, Marc Wheaton, Alec Wilder, Marianne Williamson, Travis Wilson, Bella and the Canters waitresses, and everyone at *The Young and the Restless.*

Preface

On July 14, 1989, my youngest brother beat our mother to death with a baseball bat.

This book is a record in words and images of my need to understand why she was killed. The search was debilitating and caused me to doubt my own sanity. It was also exhilarating and, I believe, miraculous.

Me, Mom, and Troy (a month before Troy killed Mom)

All events in this book are true.
Some names have been changed to protect identities.

1

Cages

That Saturday afternoon, when the phone rang with news that would change the rest of my life, I was in a monkey cage.

I had built the cage for a little Rhesus monkey named Abu. I wanted him to have as much room as possible to swing on his toy tire, so the cage extended from my bedroom window a few yards to the driveway. It was a good thing I had this extra space because when I was inside this cage, washing monkey feces off the wood slats, and stepped too close to my pet, he would back into a corner and scream. This monkey seemed to fear me from the day we met. Abu rejected most attempts to love him, and his hostility tested my affection for him daily.

The phone rang again then the machine answered.

"Tommy?" It was Hope, my 28-year-old sister.

Although I was a year younger than Hope, I felt older because I'd escaped our little midwestern town years ago. I was flying high in Hollywood, banking on my fame as a daytime TV star to propel me to my ultimate dream of movie-stardom. I might not look like Tom Cruise with my hands dripping soap scum and monkey shit, but people told me I resembled him. My look and determination landed me a big part on the country's #1 soap opera, *The Young and the Restless*. As far as I was concerned, there was nothing to stop me from becoming the next big box-office star in 1990 or soon after.

8

Hope's soft voice cracked, "Something's happened here. We have to talk."

Surprised by her tone, I quickly climbed through the window into my bedroom, dried my hands, and picked up the phone. "What's wrong?"

"He did it," Hope said. "Troy killed her."

"What?"

"Mom's dead."

"Troy killed her?"

"He killed her," she confirmed.

"Now wait a minute," I took a breath, letting it sink in. "Mom's dead?"

"He killed her." She stopped breathing.

"Are you okay?" I asked.

"I'm okay. He beat Mom's head."

Her usually cheerful husband sounded frantic as he got on the phone. "Hey, Thom, it's Sam."

"Tell Thom how," Hope quietly said in the background.

Mentally disassociating from what I was hearing, I became hypersensitive to the phone in my hand. The receiver suddenly seemed heavier, and I discovered tiny holes I'd never before noticed.

My distraction suddenly ended as Sam said, "Your brother beat her with a baseball bat. Your grandpa and cousin John found your mom this morning in her kitchen." He paused before adding, "Her head wasn't even in one piece."

My sister took the phone back. "The police say he's coming to California to get you. He wants to kill you. So you'd better get away from your house right now," she ordered. "I mean it."

2

Damn Angel

July 15, 1989

I hung up the phone and sat on the bed.

Outside the window, I could see my dark-haired lover of about a year, Rod Meyers, stop sweeping the driveway so he could play with Abu through the bars of his cage. Rod must not have heard Hope's message. I caught Rod's sensitive brown eyes, but did not cry out for him, so his attention returned to the monkey. As much as Abu loathed me, he adored Rod.

I began hunting for a message saved on the machine.

"It's just me," said Mom's voice from a few days earlier, trying to sound happier than she was. "You owe me quite a few phone calls. I want to talk to you."

What was it she wanted to talk about?

Mom's voice said, "I love you, you know," then hung up.

Was that the last message I would ever receive from my mother?

Would it be possible for my dead mother to ever get another message to me?

Could someone that was dead ever make contact again with someone alive?

Dazed, I got off the bed and walked into the bathroom. I studied my reflection in the mirror as I washed my hands. I looked different. Something was different. Something was "off." My eyes were "off."

But what about Mom's eyes? What was she looking at? Instead of watching over me from Wisconsin, I hoped she was now watching over me from somewhere else – from another dimension.

But was she farther away from me? Or closer?

I went out the bedroom's French doors into the yard and stood near Rod. His short beard and sideburns curled in the summer humidity.

"Troy killed Mom," I said matter-of-factly.

"You're kidding."

"No."

"What?!"

"Hope just called."

"No way."

"The cops say he might be coming to kill me next."

"This is a bad joke."

"Troy is probably coming after me. Or maybe he's coming after Hope or Gregg or maybe even going to try to kill Dad in Texas? Do you think he hates Dad?"

"I don't know."

"He's probably coming here. That's what Hope and the police think. He used to live here! We should warn the neighbors," I said. "They might see him climbing over our fence."

Realizing I was serious, Rod opened his arms to me. Feeling numb inside and out, I didn't want to be touched. He stared after me as I headed down the driveway. I tripped over a shingle from the roof. "Damn it! Why the fuck do these shingles fall off? Damn it!" I cursed it.

Damn angel, too.

When we began remodeling my old house, I had wired a stone angel to the chimney. My intention was for the angel to protect the house and everything in it. The angel had not done so. It hadn't even protected the roof. The twisting, thorny branches of the climbing bougainvillea plant seemed to go out of their way to dismantle any cable or antennae in their path. This insatiable plant seemed to be unusually cruel to the old and lazy sun-damaged shingles in its way, piercing and ripping them indiscriminately. Every day I encountered a new pile of dead shingles in the path of

11

my front door. Half the time I'd curse at the dead shingle itself, belittling it for not holding on longer, harder, like I imagined I would have. Then I'd toss it back up on the roof to aggravate its predator. Or if I were in a better mood, I'd laugh off the mess at my front door, pocketing the shingles until I found a garbage can. Walking around Hollywood with pieces of my roof in my back pocket, proved to be, at the very least, interesting. More interesting, however, was the fact that my home, as bright and sweet and angelic as it seemed, was coming apart at the seams.

After this outburst, my preternatural calm returned as I informed the neighbors about my mother's murder, and my brother's threat. Their expressions told me that they were unnerved by my lack of emotion.

"I never believed that human beings just die. Mom's alive somewhere else now," I said; unaware how far in denial I sounded. "I wanted you to know because Troy used to say he wanted to go out in a blood bath, so if you hear or see something, call the cops."

When I returned to my house, Rod was out front petting Abu. Rod followed me inside. I called a few friends, all of whom had met my mother and liked her. I explained that she was dead and Troy was coming for me. One friend immediately came over with a gun. I had never held a gun and didn't want one in my home. I told him to take it away. He insisted I get a bodyguard for my mother's funeral in Wisconsin. He had a friend who would do it as a favor. I stopped asking questions and agreed. I could use a bodyguard in Wisconsin; my whole family could use one as a matter of fact. I could've used one in L.A. too, fearing Troy might be outside hiding in the bushes aiming a gun - like the one I didn't want - right at me.

That night I figured Rod and I would be easy targets for Troy's attack if we were lying in our bed, so we climbed into the bedroom loft, armed with an ax. There was a fright in Rod's eyes that I had never before seen. I used to feel safe next to him, but at that moment he didn't have any way to comfort me. I lay awake absolutely still, terrified, my mind flashing on the previous year when one of Troy's psychiatrists called to warn me that I was the person Troy most often fantasized about killing.

Dean Carbian, ACSW Clinical Coordinator, Community Support Program

Troy...described how he would kill Thom slowly over about four days, torturing him. He stated he would hang him from his hands, burn him with cigarettes, pound nails into his kneecaps, use a car battery to give him electrical shocks...

"SELF-PORTRAIT IN FEAR AND LOSS"

3

On The Run

July 16 to July 18, 1989

Troy was still on the loose the next morning. The police called, urging me to leave my house immediately. The night of my mother's murder, her car was seen on the highway speeding out of Kenosha. The driver stopped, picked up a hitchhiker, and then took off again, dumping the contents of Mom's purse out the window.

My mother's credit card was traced to a Kmart near Chicago, where Troy bought spray-paint, probably to disguise our mother's car. We would later learn that Troy and the hitchhiker also switched license plates with another car in the store's parking lot.

A couple of hours further south in Illinois, Troy stopped at a phone booth and called 911. He said, "This is Thom Bierdz, the soap opera star, and I just killed my mother and raped my little brother Troy."

Troy's threats and violence had escalated for years, and I never took any of them seriously - but this manipulative behavior was something I'd never before seen from him. His attempt to frame me proved he was determined to hurt me in any way possible. When my sister told me about Troy's call, I was stunned by his audacity, and his stupidity, in thinking people would believe him.

Growing up, I rarely touched Troy. I certainly never touched him in a sexual way, and I wondered if his charge might reveal his own repressed homosexual feelings – of which I had absolutely no evidence.

Rod and I took cover at several friends' homes, including that of Jeanne Cooper, star of *The Young and the Restless*. She played Katherine

Chancellor, the widow of my character's father. Jeanne was maternal to me both onscreen and off, and she had met Troy a couple of times when I'd taken him to the CBS set. She couldn't believe he killed Mom, who many times had relaxed between scenes in Jeanne's dressing room with me.

I didn't want to endanger any of our friends by staying in one place too long, so Rod and I kept moving. Our next stop was the home of comedy actor Jim J. Bullock, who played Monroe on *Too Close for Comfort,* where my best friend Bruce Dent, also an actor and comedian, was renting a room.

From there I called Hope, anxious for news of Troy's whereabouts. She did have news, but not the kind I wanted. My head began to ache as she told me the murder was on the front page of the *Kenosha News*. This wasn't the type of fame I wanted, but it might have been just the notoriety that Troy craved.

As Hope read the news story to me, I focused on her surprisingly calm voice instead of the words. Hope had always seemed fragile to me, and although she stood two inches higher than our five-foot-tall mother, she lacked Mom's fiery spirit. My sister's small, unblemished face was as pretty as a porcelain doll, but not a doll that would be the center of attention. Her eyes were hazel brown instead of deep green, like our brother Gregg's. Her hair was also brown and usually cut at her neck. Her straight bangs occasionally touched her faint eyebrows. Her mouth was small and, like Mom, she never wore lipstick or any other make-up. There was nothing showy about her clothes. Though Hope was a natural beauty, nothing about her face was unusual, except how pink her cheeks became when she laughed – as if she was embarrassed to laugh – like she didn't have the right. As the oldest child and only girl, my sister was raised not to have fun, but to be polite, care for others, and never cause any problems. Just like the old-fashioned doll she resembled, Hope was content to exist on a shelf and watch life from a safe distance.

But how does a doll not crack into pieces when her shelf crashes to the floor? And when someone like Hope cracked into pieces, how was I supposed to put her back together?

KENOSHA NEWS:

Phyllis Bierdz, 49, was found dead in her home Saturday, apparently bludgeoned in the head by what is believed to be a blunt instrument...

Police are looking for Bierdz's youngest son, Troy, 19, for questioning. Neighbors saw him with his mother at the home Friday evening.

Bierdz's two other sons, Thom, 27, and Gregg, 25, live in California...

Bierdz's 1980 two-door tan Buick Regal is missing and a nationwide alert has been put out for the car...

[Phyllis] Bierdz had worked third shift at The Public Safety Building. She worked in the Joint Services records department, which serves the Police and Sheriff's departments...

Raymond Gramm, director of Joint Services, said she was "an excellent worker. Everybody liked her. She was a genuinely nice person."

Kenosha Police Lt. Robert F. Reschke said Phyllis Bierdz "was very bubbly. You would never know she had problems. She always put on a happy face. All this trouble the kid gave her, she always stood by him."

My sister urged Rod and me into a motel for the night. We figured Troy might be smart enough to find us at a place near my home, so we drove a few miles east on Sunset Boulevard to find a less trackable hideaway.

In the humid hotel room, Rod pulled the curtains closed, and sat in the dark playing with Abu. Rod offered to embrace me, as it was obvious that in those minutes I craved warmth. But I didn't crave his warmth; I craved my mother's warmth. Instead I took a bath, submerging myself in hot water. Keeping the scalding water dripping steadily intensified the heat in my artificial womb.

I heard a noise outside the room and froze in fear. A child giggled, then I heard her running down the hall, laughing loudly. I relaxed.

Rod sat next to the tub.

We talked about death.

Then we talked about siblings, as Rod did not get along with any of his.

Rod said, "The mother is the glue that holds the family together. If my mom doesn't make us get together, we don't. When the glue is removed, the family falls completely apart."

I wondered if that were true.

I wondered about charismatic, extroverted Gregg, who had his own apartment in Los Angeles, and shy, old-fashioned Hope – and our forecast as siblings. It's not like we'd have much in common without our mother pulling us together for the holidays. Would we even make the effort to see each other or talk? And would I even care if we became estranged? No one had ever accused me of being a "family man."

As it was, Gregg and I had nothing to say to each other since Hope had phoned each of us about Mom's death. He and I talked on the phone only to set up flights. I inquired as to his state of mind, and he wouldn't share his honest feelings of loss with me. All he said was that he wanted to kill Troy with his own hands. My mom was killed too, but I didn't want to physically kill or even hurt Troy. More violence seemed like more insanity. Gregg and I felt and thought very differently about many subjects. My handsome, heterosexual, Hollywood-networking brother and I didn't have much in common – besides the Hollywood part.

Rod, fearing Troy would ambush the funeral, said he didn't want to fly back to Kenosha with me. I told him I needed him there, and he eventually agreed to go.

On our flight to Wisconsin, I sat by the window, Rod in the middle, and Gregg, looking devastated, by the aisle.

4

In The Clouds

It was about to be the quietest plane ride of my life. Rod was desperately trying to get some sleep, and I was desperately trying to say to Gregg whatever a big brother says to his younger brother when their mother is murdered. But nothing came to mind, other than telling him that I knew Mom loved him very much.

I also loved my brother Gregg, and usually I wanted to be him. He projected confidence and freedom – qualities that seemed alien to me. It was like we were from different planets. I never felt the magnetic, united bond of brethren toward Gregg that I had imagined since I was a young boy that I should feel. And I know he didn't feel it toward me.

Gregg didn't understand my choices, my lifestyle, my artistic nature, my honesty, my anxiety, and my over-sharing. He didn't appreciate my advice. We didn't even look alike, the way Troy and I did.

As Gregg sat next to me on the plane, I didn't know his thoughts about our mother. But I saw Gregg's frown deepen and his masculine profile increase in age by ten years. His green eyes searched the plane, noticing pretty women, but that day only out of habit. Gregg appeared to be hurting badly. Mom's tragic death was probably the beginning of Gregg's alopecia: a stress disease that caused chunks of his hair to fall out.

Did Gregg fear the rumor we'd heard that Troy planned to greet us with a machine gun as we landed? Was Gregg wondering, as I was, whom Troy would shoot first?

And why?

Gregg and Troy never got along, but Troy didn't get along with anyone in the family. Still, to my knowledge, Troy had never singled out wanting to kill Gregg as he had me.

Did Troy hate Gregg less because they were both straight?

Did Troy hate me more because I was gay?

Or did Troy hate me more because I was "famous?" I had some evidence he might. The year before this flight, Troy was committed to a psychiatric hospital in Kenosha. An acquaintance and his brother visited Troy at the hospital. The police questioned this acquaintance after Troy escaped by assaulting a nurse.

10/20/88 POLICE STATEMENT:

"Troy was in the lounge area, Troy was telling my brother Steve how he (Troy) was going to break out of the hospital and kill his brother the actor. I told Troy quit talking to my brother like that because he's only 14-years-old."

5

A Kenosha Miracle

1960 to 1970

On the five-hour flight to Wisconsin, I had time to dwell upon the thoughts I'd been distracted from the past few days. Until we landed, I was temporarily safe from Troy's threats. I began reviewing my life, and what I knew of Troy's, trying to figure out why he did the unspeakable to our mother. As the hours passed, my mind moved back in time to before Troy's birth and my birth – to the things I only knew from other people's memories.

• • •

Northern Europeans were the first Caucasian settlers of this lush territory, shipping off to reservations by any means necessary the indigenous Native Americans. Kenosha began primarily as dairy farms and scenic ports on Lake Michigan. The town, just over the state line from Illinois, seemed destined to become an industrial superb of Chicago. When the African-Americans, and even the Jews and Italians, arrived in Kenosha, the original white farmers could not get rid of them as easily as the Indians. In 1940, this was the world my olive-skinned Italian mother was born into. My fair-skinned Polish father, on the other hand, did not suffer any prejudice. However, his parents, friendly Polish stock, were not thrilled when he took an Italian as a bride.

In the 1950s, long stretches of cattle fences gave way to factories like American Motors: makers of Javelins, Hornets, Ramblers, and Gremlins.

At the end of their long shifts, most assembly workers, earning minimum wage, flooded into corner taverns for a stein of Old Milwaukee beer. Instead, both my grandfathers always went straight home to their wives; a cold beer wasn't worth a hot fight.

By the 1980s, the suburbs of Chicago and Milwaukee were severely encroaching on Kenosha. Hundreds of condos, a marina, and a spacious outdoor mall were added near the lake. The I-94 freeway, bordering the west side of Kenosha, sported a new greyhound racetrack, more condos, and an adult bookstore. These "improvements" looked out of place between red barns, silver silos, and tourist traps selling cheese.

"KENOSHA OF LORE"
(In the collection of Adrienne Kessler)

Mom was born Philomena Rachel DiLetti, but called Phyllis, and grew up to be a dark-eyed, tiny beauty. Her short black hair covered a head so small she had to wear children's hats. When people remarked about her stature, she would smile and say, "Big things come in small packages."

My father, Thomas Alexander Bierdz, Sr., also had dark hair, but his soft hazel eyes were as passive as Mom's dark ones were engaging. Their eyes perfectly summed up their differing temperaments; he observed and commented from a distance, while she loved, laughed, held, argued, and cried in your face.

My introverted father dreamed of becoming an actor. He rarely told people that in 1960 he was accepted at the renowned Pasadena Playhouse in California, because he had chickened-out of going there. Raised by an over-protective mother, who never even let him spend an evening out with relatives, he lacked confidence to venture out on his own. So the 21-year-old tossed his dream out the window and did the expected: he married his passionate 19-year-old girlfriend who gave birth to my sister the following year. Part of me wondered if I, born the next year in 1962, had crawled outside that window and gotten my hands on his discarded Hollywood dream.

Regretting not pursuing his showbiz dream, Dad was determined to be a success in another vocation. He eventually studied psychotherapy and earned a master's degree.

Mom made big sacrifices to support him while he attended a Chicago university. The only apartment they could afford in a very dangerous neighborhood. For our safety, Mom was advised to lock us in the basement with her when doing laundry. She took in people's ironing to help pay bills. Her mother taught her how to make meatballs taste expensive to satisfy Dad's college friends when they came over. Mom felt left out, like all of her husband's buddies and their wives were advancing their educations and social lives, while she was imprisoned in a rough building, without any friends, and nurturing two small children. When Dad's peers weren't over for supper, Mom cooked discounted ground beef with noodles. She finally grew so sick of it, that once we left that apartment she would never again eat hamburger.

I don't remember those first two years of my life in Chicago, but I remember when Dad got his master's degree and we moved back to Kenosha. Both sets of my grandparents visited our little house and spoiled us with what they could afford. Though the Bierdzes loved us and made Sunday lunches after we went to St. Mark's Church, the DiLettis were more generous with physical affection and daily help. Grandma DiLetti, with dyed-red hair, spent all day playing Match Box cars with us on the rug, while my mother waitressed and my father worked as a social worker. On weekends, short Grandpa DiLetti, with a round head and little hook-nose like an owl, helped my father fix up our basement. My mother called her parents "saints." I understood this to mean that the harder someone worked, the closer they were to God. The Almighty obviously wanted people to work.

With the work it took to sew her own clothes and ours, I imagined my mother was in very good standing with God. I often fell asleep to the comforting sound of her foot-pump sewing machine whirring at top speed. She'd put out her Pall Mall cigarette and carry me to bed.

In 1964, I had a baby brother named Gregg and a Pekinese-poodle named Sassy. I would pet Sassy for hours, even though I had allergies to all pets; allergies that would worsen as I aged, requiring me to use an inhaler. When Sassy lay on her side, I liked to hold her paws. I suppose the texture and heat of her paw pads felt more human than her fluffy sandy-colored hair. We watched *Lost in Space* together. Sassy knew how much I wanted to be boy astronaut Will Robinson, who flew to planets with his family and a robot. I felt a great connection with Sassy, like we communicated without words.

As a small boy, I needed an animal confidant because I did not trust people. I thought everyone was a robot and that they were out to kill me. I was unsure about why they wanted to kill me, but I reasoned that if I were polite and perfect and caused them no trouble they might let me live. I remained on my best behavior - reserved and on guard - never letting anyone get too close.

I don't know if I was born paranoid, or if I was subconsciously influenced by the spooky movies and TV shows my mother loved watching. Doting Mom was the one human I believed wasn't a robot, maybe because she "clued" me into the conspiracy with episodes of *The Twilight Zone* and *Outer Limits*. My sister was the only other person I didn't fear; although she might have been a robot, I was sure she couldn't outsmart me.

Sassy's and my silent, soulful conversations and confessions increased as I turned three, then four, then five. Since robots were watching and listening all the time, I couldn't risk whispering the truth to Mom. Without me telling her, she seemed to understand how important I was, that the whole world was focused on me. Occasionally, I would forget about this omnipotent attention, and could laugh and play almost like a "normal" kid. At these times, however, the paranoia was only buried, not extinguished, and would show itself in my nightmares.

"PARANOID IN RED AND BLUE"

25

This fear remained with me until I was six or seven, when I realized that if everyone *were* a robot, they already would have "gotten" me. I never told anyone but Sassy about this paranoia. As an adult, I would wonder how this psychosis played into me being a "performer." Why did I feel compelled, obligated even, to be watched?

By the late 1960s, raising three kids and a dog had strained my parents' marriage and destroyed their youthful romance. My father was now a respected psychotherapist and too distracted by raising his patients' consciousness to be much help raising his own children. As he successfully counseled these patients along the path to inner peace and freedom, he may have inadvertently followed them.

Mom and Dad separated twice by the time I was eight. Both times my happy mother disappeared and was replaced by one whose constant focus on her children bordered on obsessive. I felt especially singled out for her attention. As she fussed with my hair and my exaggerated shirt collars, I would smell the ivory soap on her face and stare into her disappointed eyes. Standing so close to her I could tell exactly what shade of brown her eyes were: sepia-brown. And I had the crayon to prove it in my treasured box of sixty-four Crayola crayons. I attempted to absorb the pain and disillusionment in my mother's sepia-brown eyes, just like Sassy absorbed my hurt. Sassy could absolve my troubles without being affected, but I never learned that trick. Instead I took on Mom's heartache, becoming more withdrawn and frustrated each time Dad left.

Our parents' separations also changed my sister Hope, as she lost confidence and her spirit appeared to me to be forever broken. Like me, Hope went to great lengths to ease our mother's sadness by concealing her own suffering. She developed the lifelong habit of crying secretly, alone in the bathroom or her bedroom. Only our younger brother Gregg appeared unaffected; his sunny disposition unaltered.

A few weeks after leaving, our father would once again do what he was expected to do - what he was told to do - and return. Just as he followed Grandma Bierdz's urging to give up his acting dream, settle in Kenosha, marry, and raise a family, he listened to Grandma's lectures that a marriage vow was sacred and must be upheld. "No ifs, ands or buts." "Family comes first."

Each time Dad came back to us, Mom's loving devotion to him would return. She would stop nagging him, and he offered to do more around the house. Our family operated better with Dad home, but there was a problem: he wasn't in love with her anymore.

A second problem was Mom wanted another baby, possibly to tie my father down more permanently. Dad knew a fourth child was a bad idea, but he also believed she couldn't get pregnant again because her doctor said she had a tipped uterus. Due to this condition, Dad did not insist on using birth control, even though he didn't want any more children.

I don't know if Mom prayed to God, Jesus, the Holy Mother, or any of the many Catholic saints to give her a baby, but based upon the strength of her religious beliefs, I would not be surprised if she lit a candle. If she did ask for divine intervention, her prayers were answered in late 1969; she was miraculously pregnant.

That winter, her belly was huge against her small body. She could barely squeeze between the kitchen counters when she made fresh-buttered popcorn for my brother, sister, and me as we played cards. She was all smiles again.

Troy was born on April 15, 1970. Mom called him her miracle baby.

"MADONNA AND CHILD"

6

Penance To Be Perfect

EVIL IN SEASON
Evil in season
Taste the blood
Churn the knife
Start the flood
Kill the pigs
Slaughter them all
Stack them up
Stack them tall
A quest for me?
We soon shall see.
—TROY BIERDZ (at 17)

1970 to 1975

Ididn't think Troy was a miracle. I thought he was a pest. Playing alone in the basement as a boy, I loved to create cities built from Legos and Lincoln Logs with Hot Wheels track streets and highways traveled by my treasured Match Box cars. Troy would try to play with my toys, but would inadvertently crash onto them like some baby Godzilla monster, trampling to bits my carefully constructed fantasy city.

This little miracle was usually clinging to our mother's legs, or annoyingly following around one of us siblings. When I was petting Sassy, and telling her that I wanted to run away to Hollywood to be a TV star like Mike Conners of *Mannix*, Troy would be right in my face wanting to pet Sassy, too.

So, I would have to move outside to the patio where my other pet was.

I was enamored with the little guinea pig in the pet store and Mom bought him for me as a birthday gift. We didn't have a cage, only a large cardboard box without a top. I don't remember his name, as we had him so briefly. I loved holding him, and was surprised to learn guinea pigs sang. He sang a very high note, when I held him in my hands. The pitch varied depending on where he was being touched – or squeezed. Apparently I was holding him too tightly, and his "songs" were actually cries of pain. I misinterpreted his crying as singing.

I kept squeezing him.

And he kept hitting higher notes.

Then, one day, the singing stopped. His lifeless body felt like a beanbag in my trembling, little hands.

I had killed my new pet.

I had killed without warning, in a split second, when I thought I was doing something good.

Everything in his sparky personality had, in fact, disappeared. All I was left with was deadness in my hands, and the hideous new information that I was a killer.

When I could not bring him back to life, I entered the house and walked to where my parents talked over the dirty supper plates. My stomach was in knots as I held my pet in my hands; he wasn't breathing, but there was no blood. I explained exactly what happened, and announced that I knew I was going to Hell. I hugged my mother delicately, as I did not want my evilness to smear or infect her. I said I didn't want to go to Hell, and that I was sorry. As she hugged me, it occurred to me why I did not want to go to Hell – because she was too good to ever go to Hell. At that point, I could not imagine ever separating from her.

• • •

That memory vanished instantly when I realized I was sitting on a plane because I had, in fact, separated from her. She was dead. Troy had killed her.

Looking out the plane window, the miniscule hills and valleys below looked like paint globs on a Jackson Pollack. I wondered what highway, what winding line of paint drizzle, Troy was on. I didn't know then that the hitchhiker was still riding with Troy. The day after picking the hitchhiker up, Troy told him that his older brother, named Thom Bierdz, had killed his mother.

The hitchhiker's response was, "Are you sure?"

Troy said yes.

The next day, Troy admitted to the hitchhiker that he was the one who killed our mother.

The hitchhiker had the same response, "Are you sure?"

Troy said yes.

On one of those highways below that looked like paint drizzle, the hitchhiker continued riding with Troy.

Why?

Where were they going?

How does someone stay in the car with a murderer?

Why does somebody murder?

When did Troy first begin to think about murdering Mom?

When did he begin to think about murdering me?

When did he begin to think about murdering?

• • •

I would later learn that when Troy was 12-years-old he wrote an essay on assassinating the president of the United States. The thought of killing had been in his head constantly after that. In his own words: "For the publicity or in a manner of gaining manhood."

I couldn't relate to Troy's adolescent aggression. I was a very mild-

31

mannered, polite, robot-fearing boy. When I was 12, my idea of manhood was my father, and I wanted to be him in every way.

It was when I was 12 that Dad took me into my parents' bedroom to explain divorce. He said he was leaving because my mother was overly controlling, and he felt like he was suffocating. Apparently, he didn't remember that when he went to college, he asked his inexperienced, petite, teenage bride to raise small kids in a dangerous Chicago neighborhood, and needed her to be in control. And he needed her to be in control when they had two more kids. And he had needed her to be in control of all their household responsibilities each day when he was at work, attaining his financial success, admiration, and even adulation from patients.

As unfair as it was, my angel of a mother had been deserted, because my father "needed space."

My mother made me choose sides, and I chose hers. She became my new father.

She was my father, my mother, and my martyr.

I learned a new feeling: loneliness. Her loneliness. It ached inside my ribcage. Was as heavy as a bowling ball. I learned what it was like to be abandoned. As a 12-year-old boy, I learned *dire* frustration. I was frustrated there was the same likelihood of bringing my father back home as there was of restoring my guinea pig to life.

I had to settle for seeing my father every other Saturday. If he took us to an upscale restaurant like the Midtown Bar and Grill, we were coaxed to split an expensive meatball sandwich because we could rarely finish the whole thing alone. But we would make fun of his frugality afterward to Mom, and we'd ridicule his suit pants that were several inches too short. Mom would boastingly take us to the Midtown another time, and order us each whole meatball bombers. Because she had to roll pennies to pay the check, she was a "saint." Our father, consequently, was a "sinner," a "bad guy," an "irresponsible father" with high-waters for pants, and, if we believed our mother, a "hypocrite" to be a family therapist.

My overburdened mother waitressed part-time at The Ranch restaurant and, in addition, clerked part-time at the Kenosha Safety Building.

Dad's child-support checks were often late because he was behind on his own expenses. Though she needed more money, my mother was most assuredly a fighter and her pride stopped her from pressing the court to ask Dad to send her alimony. I learned from Mom that the more someone struggles, and the poorer they were, the *better* they were as people. Her behavior taught me that rich people shouldn't be trusted. And people trying to get rich, or acting like they had money, were just plain suspicious.

Two jobs and raising four kids – alone – was too much for her. I felt it. I saw it in her eyes.

SATAN
His name is only whispered
his number seldom found.
I find his soul within me,
hes learking all around.
He's in us all,
we live his life.
We see his feats of SACRIFICE!!
We must dream on,
we must see through
To find his everlasting clue.
He is our creator,
our master in a way.
EVIL & DESTRUCTION
SORCERY & PAIN –
– TROY BIERDZ (at 18)

I figured it was time for me to be a "man" – or a martyr – and struggle with a job too, so I became a paperboy for the Sunday *Milwaukee Journal*.

Mom helped me deliver these heavy papers when she could. Afterwards we would go to church. St. Mark's Church was enormous and modern, round with orange carpeting. The stained glass windows were fifty-feet-high.

I hated that my mother put money in the offertory basket each week. It was then I first suspected St. Mark's wasn't in good communication with the real God, because I figured the real God knew she needed the money more than the church needed it. It's not like *we* had brand new orange carpeting at home. We didn't have orange anything. And if anyone noticed colors, it was me – thanks to the regular use of my deluxe box of sixty-four Crayola crayons.

Ours was an ordinary kitchen with the then-popular copper spray-painted refrigerator with black spray-painted border and matching stove. She had chosen gold wallpaper with crimson horse drawn carriages for the walls. It was ironic that the wallpaper suggested so much movement when my mother seemed fated to be stuck at that home.

I learned many things in that kitchen at 12-years-old. I learned to chew my Cap'n Crunch cereal as quietly as possible. The Cap'n did not design his cereal to bother mothers who needed a "moment of silence, kiddo."

Gregg, then 10-years-old, crunched loudly. He was as beautiful as a blond kid on a suntan commercial. I learned I was envious of Gregg's green eyes. More specifically – thanks to my box of crayons – I envied his pine green eyes. I learned I was jealous of his happy-go-lucky spirit. I envied Gregg for playing Little League Baseball, because we had tried out together, and I, the older brother, failed to make the team.

So, I excelled in areas my siblings couldn't, like getting straight A's in school. It wasn't easy; I had to challenge my concentration skills in all my classes to achieve that, except one – art class. Amazingly, when I had a paintbrush in my hand, I did the opposite of concentrate; I stopped thinking altogether. Strangely enough, my teacher encouraged this lack of thought. He taped my paintings to the walls every week, as an example for other students to emulate, remarking that I had an innate sense of composition that couldn't be taught (not that I had any idea what he was talking about). He also told the class, he wanted to acknowledge me

Forgiving Troy

for painting so quickly and with such "faith." He hoped the other students would learn to trust their instincts more, instead of second-guessing their brushstrokes.

My parents' friends also praised me for my artwork that Mom posted on our refrigerator, as much as they praised Gregg for sports. I was even awarded with a special art school vacation by the entire board of teachers for my work as Captain of Patrol. My job was to walk, usually in the snow, the six blocks of street corners surrounding the elementary school, making sure the other crossing guards showed up for duty.

I was very serious about being the best little robot I could be.

Too serious.

The Wisconsin Dairy Board, promoting healthy diets, asked students to fill out breakfast questionnaires. We were encouraged to have balanced meals made up of the four food groups: meat, fruits and vegetables, grains and cereals, and, most importantly in cattle country, dairy. The questionnaire stated that we should put a check in the box next to the name of the food that we had eaten that morning. Choices included oatmeal, cream of wheat, assorted cold cereals, waffles, pancakes, toast, French toast, Pop Tarts, eggs, bacon, sausage, ham, hamburger patty, melon, grapefruit, bananas, orange juice, grapefruit juice, tomato juice, milk, chocolate milk, skim milk, yogurt, sour cream, butter, whipped cream, potatoes, tomatoes, onions, peppers, mushrooms, etc.

I checked the box next to cereal for Cap'n Crunch. Then, mistaking this form to be a test one could fail, and I did not want to fail any test – I wanted to be perfect – adored – trouble-free – I checked everything else. I checked that I had eaten *over thirty items that morning.*

After school, the teacher, Mrs. Gallo, sat down next to me and asked if I understood the questionnaire. Stammering guiltily, I insisted I ate everything on the list that morning. And if I had the chance to turn the clock back, I would have eaten everything to save face. I hated lying. It was a horrible feeling. Like motion sickness with a headache.

I wouldn't have lied if I knew we would be getting the same questionnaire the next day. I felt obligated to check all the boxes again, as the other students' eyes watched in what I believed was awe. I was too embarrassed to change my story on the second day. Or the third. Or the fourth. Or the fourth week. Or the fourth month.

Being a good kid was work. A lot of work. A lot of manipulation.

I was too busy appearing perfect to the entire school body to have any real friends at recess. So, I settled for friends at home. Mom was my friend. Sassy was my friend.

But that wasn't enough.

Neighbor Buddy Klopstein would have been great, as I was in love with the blond Little-Leaguer, but he preferred to hang out with Gregg.

How could Gregg and I be "friends?" Gregg knew I didn't want to play catch with him in the backyard, and he didn't want to do Paint-By-Numbers with me on the kitchen table.

Hope and I were very polite kids, and "good kids," but that wasn't enough to make her my friend, per se. It's not like we could talk about how cute Buddy Klopstein was. She would squeal on me.

And Troy was just too young to be my friend. He was eight years younger than me; the "miracle" was now an erratic, screaming, manic 4-year-old.

Mom had no experience coping with a child so out-of-control. Hope, Gregg, and I rarely even misbehaved, and Mom swiftly corrected us if we did. When none of her usual methods of discipline worked on Troy, she had no choice but to bring him to the family doctor, who told Mom nothing was wrong with Troy; he was just hyperactive. Instead of medication, the doctor said all Troy needed was more attention.

This inadequate diagnosis and prescription for Troy to receive "more attention" from our recently-divorced, over-worked mother, would one day seem like a cruel, and deadly, joke.

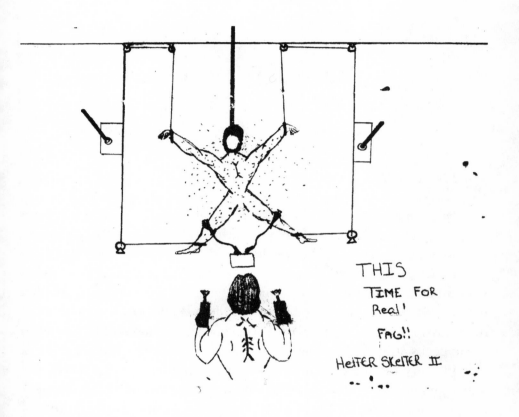

The torture drawing Troy sent to me when he was 18.

7

Racing To Racine

1975 to 1979

If round-the-clock, daily doses of our mother's attention were what 5-year-old Troy required, then his "hyperactivity" should have been cured. She watched over him – and me – constantly.

At 12, I craved Mom's attention, but at 17, I preferred to be alone with a nudie/muscle magazine. One of the "loose" divorcees in Mom's Parents-Without-Partners group insisted Mom keep a *Playgirl* in her bedroom dresser. When Mom wasn't working it was impossible for me to sneak peeks at it, because she knew what was happening with each of us kids in every room all the time. I was beginning to understand why my father said he was "suffocating" before he left. My beautiful, giving, generous, adoring, doting "Super-Mom" had transformed into "Controlling Mom." I could no longer breathe under her constant protective gaze, and there wasn't an inhaler big enough to cure this condition.

That winter, Mom tried to "ground" me because I was questioning authority – hers and society's – at every opportunity. The truth was I secretly doubted I even belonged in society, as homosexuals were considered jokes, deviant, or invisible. But I didn't tell anyone I was gay at that point, not even Mom. I couldn't bear to have her say to me that homosexuals were condemned to Hell, as my well-meaning, religious grandparents believed.

Mom clutched and shook me by my elbows, trying to hold me in place and force me to listen to her "rules." I looked down into her disapproving face, and realized for the first time how much I had outgrown her.

Suddenly, and maybe too forcefully, I took hold of her tiny forearms and freed myself from her grasp.

The phone rang. It was Grandma DiLetti with her daily soap opera recap. Regaining her composure, Mom told Grandma, "Tommy hit me." She must have believed that. But I didn't hit her. I just pushed Mom off of me, as she unwittingly personified every restriction and limitation and judgment I felt from the church and society. I was also transferring to her my anger at radio stations. I liked to listen to love songs late at night while fantasizing about adult romances, but there was not one love song on the radio without heterosexual-themed lyrics. Not one.

Confused and angry, I slipped down to my basement bedroom. I put some clothes into a duffel bag, along with the sketchpad in which daily I drew faces. Serious faces. Cowboy faces. Waitress faces. Mom's many faces. I opened the bedroom door to leave and found my mother waiting on the other side. I ran up the stairs. She chased after me and slipped. I didn't turn around.

I escaped outside into the freezing back yard and inhaled the icy wind that was rattling the chains of our rusty swing set. I wondered why our mother left it up. We weren't kids anymore. Shy 18-year-old Hope would leave soon for college. Gregg was only 15, but he was always out of the house with a girl. Even 9-year-old Troy didn't use the swing set. I wished then that Mom would forget about me completely and just concentrate on Troy, who still hung onto her at every opportunity.

If I didn't break the co-dependence I had with my mother when I did at 17, perhaps I would have hit her one day. I don't know. Was there a chance I would have even beaten her? I couldn't imagine it, but I had already been accused of having, like my mother, an "Italian temper."

My father said that at one point he wanted to kill Mom because he couldn't get away from her. He said he left because he "needed space."

I also left my mother because I "needed space."

• • •

This memory made me feel so uncomfortable and guilty that I had to shift in my seat on the plane. Rod was sound asleep; his head bobbing above his crossed arms. Gregg put down the pink piece of paper he'd been scribbling on, and turned to read an Anthony Robbins motivational book. I leaned into the window and tried to see a picture in the clouds. Nothing came to me, which was bizarre because I normally saw so many pictures, faces, buildings in clouds. My mind was typically overactive, trained for some reason, to take in something like random clouds and find a face in them. Consciously, or subconsciously, I was always trying to make sense of what didn't make sense; trying to organize things that couldn't be organized; trying to make reason out of something unreasonable, something chaotic; and searching for a purpose in things that maybe had no purpose.

Like murder.

When the clouds dissolved, I stared at the cities below, fascinated at the crisscrossing of the highways.

Wherever Troy was, he was getting "space," driving on one of those roads.

And it seemed so damn unfair.

• • •

At 17, I needed the space that I felt I would get from living with my bachelor father in his Racine apartment, half an hour north of Kenosha.

I enjoyed the freedom Dad's passivity gave me, but I resented the freedom he had in his own life, and still hated him for deserting Mom. I was old enough to sympathize with Dad needing to be unencumbered, but that didn't bring me the sense of peace I was missing as a teen. It had been easier to believe there was only one side to every issue – my mother's. But, almost an adult, I knew more, and it bothered me that life was getting complicated, and consequently there appeared to be no absolute "right" or "wrong."

On the plane ride to my mother's funeral, I decided Dad gave me more space as a teenager because he just didn't love me to the extreme Mom did. It bothered me that my ambivalent father didn't smile at me like Mom would. I didn't see his unconditional love for me in his eyes. Did he see his son in front of him, or just another patient to analyze? I didn't bond with him then like I had hoped, which is probably the reason I very much looked forward to spending weekends with my mother.

At 17, I was too embarrassed to tell either of my parents I was gay. For a few months I even dated a sweet girl named Sandy. I was not aroused when she wanted to experiment sexually. Without explaining why, I broke up with her, breaking her heart more than I realized. Though I didn't tell Sandy, Mom, or Dad I was gay, I told them my other secret: that I was going to be a movie-star.

Mom accepted it as fact, but was disappointed I would not be a priest as she felt that was my natural calling. Dad was more practical, and said I was "not tall or good-looking enough to be a movie-star." Maybe he said this out of fatherly concern to protect me, or maybe he said it out of jealousy and his own forfeited acting dream.

In any event, he underestimated my drive, or more, my need to over-compensate and be loved.

8

Cowboy Gary

1980 to 1983

When I lived at my Dad's apartment, I had plenty of alone time after school. I masturbated to pornography I stole from a neighbor's storage unit. When my guilt grew greater than the pleasure, I returned the magazines, with a note of apology.

Later, upon discovery of Troy's writings, I learned we had sexual self-hatred in common. But whereas his fantasies included *Charlie's Angels*, I had opted for *Starsky and Hutch*.

From Troy's Diary:

<u>THY SHALL NOT COVENITE THY NEIGHBORS WIFE</u>
I have had evil thoughts and have masterbated to these thought, and thoughts of these womans: Missy (greggs girlfriend), Stephanie Kramer (TV STAR), lisa Graff (sisters friend), Sheron (sisters friend) Bev, Daught (Jenny) and Bevs sister. Julie Szarafinski (school mate), nurses, porno phone sex (I called a mumeris amount of times) Cheril Lad, Kate Jackson, Fahara Fawcite, (TV STARS)

Hiding my sexuality was becoming more difficult every day. After completing high school and quickly dropping out of college, I got a job washing dishes at Mr. Steak. Due to the many derogatory comments about homosexuals from co-workers, I only came out to Gene, another gay dishwasher.

On my 18th birthday, I wrote a very anguished letter to God formally telling him I was gay – and I was planning to be a famous man in the future. I wanted God to be okay with me being famous *and* gay because I didn't want to "sin," and I didn't want to potentially influence others to sin. I hoped my grandiose future plans were all right in His book. I had a suspicion "His book" would understand love between any two people. I figured God knew how irresistible men were – didn't He make them? How could He hate me for loving what he did, and did so well?

As a declaration of my spiritual devotion, I took a new name, "TJ." People assumed it was for "Tom Junior." It secretly meant "To Jesus" – and was a daily reminder that my life should be dedicated to the highest principles.

And my life *was* dedicated to those high principles. That is, between my shifts working at Milwaukee's gay disco bars.

When I moved to Milwaukee at 19, I fell in love with Gary Scheuerman, a bearded bartender at a disco called Club 219. Gary was a tall, muscular cowboy, about fifteen years older than me, with receding blond hair that enhanced his masculinity. He looked German, and only the inner peace radiating from his Nordic blue eyes hinted that he was also half Cherokee. His Native-American past was rich with "shamans" and "spirit-walkers." I was at first skeptical, and later fascinated, to discover Gary had inherited some of his ancestor's clairvoyant abilities.

Gary lived north of Milwaukee, on a beautiful, small lake surrounded by evergreens. We would take his speedboat out on the crystal water, and it seemed like there was only the two of us in the world. Still, I was afraid to show physical displays of affection to him outdoors. Afraid someone might see.

Gary's love and confidence made me feel like a "real man" for the first time in my life. My mother, on the other hand, was determined to keep me her "little boy," even if that meant coming face to face with the realization that I was her "gay little boy."

When I first asked Mom to meet Gary she seemed hesitant. I may have hoped introducing them at Club 219, instead of some neutral location, would intimidate my tiny mother, but she marched up to my towering, hairy-chested cowboy as the disco hit *It's Raining Men* bellowed, ordered

Thom Bierdz

"INDIAN SPIRIT GUIDE"

44

a drink, then ordered him to take good care of me. Gary promised he would, and in time Mom gave us her blessing.

Gary did take good care of me. He helped me get a job bartending at a gay bar named Your Place, and also at Club 219.

From the time I was 19 until my 21st birthday, customers knew me as "TJ" in the tan cowboy hat, strutting behind the bar to disco hits like *Funky Town*. It was bizarre how quickly I transformed into this new, freer, more-confident personality. Where had this persona come from? Was he buried inside me all this time? Or was he invented; in essence, my first recurring acting role?

I tried growing something like a mustache and wore tight T-shirts to expose the biceps I developed at a gym. When my muscles didn't grow as quickly as I wanted, I bought tighter T-shirts. Every night I'd be complimented, and propositioned. I must have appeared conceited because one customer whispered that I "needed to learn humility."

"TJ" may have been my new personality, but robot-fearing "Tommy" reappeared after about three hours with all his insecurities and neurosis in check. To escape "Tommy," I needed more than the compliments and propositions – I needed shots of Peppermint Schnapps.

Gary and I, both popular bartenders, shared a happy on-and-off again relationship until I turned 21 and left for Hollywood. That had been my plan, and five-thousand-dollars in tips from admiring customers gave me just enough money to follow it.

As I was leaving, Gary said, "You came to Milwaukee and made a name for yourself. You'll do the same thing in Hollywood, Teej. I know you will."

"I have to go for it," I said, adjusting his cowboy hat.

He smiled and straightened *my* cowboy hat, "You will do more than 'go for it.' You will do it. You'll get work as an actor. I can see it. Really. Like you're on screen already."

Besides my mother, Gary was the only other person to share my dream, who believed I would really achieve it, and as he watched me fly away, he was still keeping his promise to take good care of me.

9

Troy Reaches Puberty

1983 to 1985

After arriving in Hollywood, I found a very cheap apartment in neighboring Silverlake. Coming from Wisconsin, I had never seen a chain-link fence encircling a reservoir of water. This small excuse for a "lake" looked imprisoned and unattractive to me, but the Californians loved it so much they built million-dollar homes around it.

While working as a restaurant busboy, I was "discovered" and introduced to Tim Wood, Rob Lowe's manager. Tim took me on as a client, arranged my headshots and acting classes, and changed my name from "TJ Bierdz" or "Tom Bierdz, Jr." to "Thom Bierdz." Thanks to his help, I landed my first commercial audition and got the part. I was a principle in a Dr. Pepper spot that was filmed across from Paramount Studios at Raleigh Studios. A few other small roles came my way over the next year but I still had to wait tables until my "big break."

Back in Wisconsin, Mom was still working two jobs and barely making ends meet. By 1984, my 23-year-old sister Hope had finally moved out and into an apartment by Parkside College. She was a devoted student studying business administration, and she appreciated our mother's financial help for tuition. I too welcomed the small checks my mother sent for acting classes. Gregg, 20, was living in upstate Wisconsin at the University of Eau Claire. I imagine my carefree blond brother was not only living, but also "living it up." The money our Mother sent to Gregg for tuition went for pizza and beer. And Troy was always expensive to raise.

Emotionally expensive.

The onset of puberty, and new raging hormones, had turned Mom's clingy little boy into someone withdrawn, awkward, offbeat, secretly aggressive, secretly paranoid, and, of course, secretly going to Hell for masturbating.

From Troy's Diary:

<u>THY SHALL NOT COVENITE THY NEIGHBORS WIFE</u>
I have had evil thoughts and have masterbated to these thought,
and thoughts of these womans: woman I have seen on the streets,
Vanessa (classmate), CANDY (ex-girlfriend), Lonie Anderson
(TV STAR), Eva Torrez, posters of woman...Tracy Heison,
Belinda Carliel, Just about every woman I saw.

14-year-old Troy didn't socialize with the girls – or boys – at Lincoln Junior High School. And some for good reason, as racial tensions divided the whites and blacks into gangs. Longhaired Troy avoided gangs of any sort, and hid his insecurity and fear of groups behind a rough exterior, a scowling face to mask his good looks, and an intimidating walk overcompensating for his thin body type.

He kept to himself and engaged friends one at a time. People assumed he was spacing out in a corner of the back row as he stared at insects on the floor for minutes at a time, as though trying to extract some communication from the bug itself. And one might think Troy squashed the bugs slowly, methodically, because he wasn't satisfied with the communication. But he had another agenda.

As the class spied on my brother pulling the legs off insects, he was spying on the class, searching specifically for a reaction of mild indifference. The faces registering disgust and squeamishness, he kept at a distance. These kids would not make good followers. They wouldn't understand him. They'd question him. Troy didn't want to be questioned.

The loud rebels who applauded and grinned at Troy's insect squashing were useless to him as well. These dissidents could look him in the eye. And though their stares were supportive, they might later turn against him. Anybody who could lock eyes with him contained some measure of guts; he didn't want to deal with anybody else's guts.

Only the weak indifferent smirkers were allowed closer, one at a time, to this quiet anarchist. Maybe this was because Troy needed just one follower at a time. Or maybe it was because exposing himself was an excruciating ordeal. There was only one ordeal more excruciating – being completely alone.

When he was alone he had to deal with his destructive fantasies. He engaged them half the time, and resisted them as often.

So my brother, the quiet bug crusher, remained out of bounds to everyone, but the brain-dead. Possibly, if he had been secure enough to allow into his space someone with a working mind, he could've been steered out of his pattern to crush. I do not know. For his own reasons, Troy felt separated. He was a loner.

From Troy's Diary:

I pulled a knife on Richard Heckel – I was prejudist (I spray painted on the back of checkers) I have made weapons, such as nunchucks, tenfas. I have carried knifes intending to do harm to myself as well as others. I have made bats and pounded nails threw them, intending to do harm to others in gangfights. Evil thoughts of Joining cults!

Shortly before turning 15, Troy was informed he would not be allowed on the wrestling team, because he had been suspended from school too many times. Retaliating, he kicked in several of the school's glass doors.

Later that night, Troy stole our mother's Buick and picked up his current follower of choice, Kevin Patterson, a lanky redheaded burnout. They circled the high school, pumping the accelerator, spinning, and making as big a scene as possible.

Phone in hand, our mother paced her kitchen wondering what to do. Troy had never taken the car before. She didn't even know he could drive. For his safety, she called the police department.

Troy returned forty-five minutes later, before the police arrived. Mom didn't file charges.

Since Troy's first suspension six months earlier, she had taken him to a series of counselors. However, this therapy didn't seem to be reducing his aggression.

With Gregg away at college, and our father out of the picture, our mother thought Troy needed a stabilizing, masculine presence in his life. Partly for his benefit, she began dating Chip Nagel, an easygoing guy with corny jokes who liked kids. Chip was also an unemployed, divorced man who loved spending his days golfing, and afternoons in taverns.

When Mom wasn't needling Chip to get a job, she enjoyed sunny Sundays with him on the putting green. For the first time since her divorce a decade before, she was enjoying chemistry with a man. She was allowing herself to fall in love. But she didn't tell Chip yet. She wouldn't tell him until she knew for certain that he would be a good influence on Troy.

Because of the damage Troy caused to the school's doors, the education board filed charges for criminal damage and truancy. Against our mother's wishes, Troy was sentenced to live for nine months at Shelter Care, a supervised citywide organization for the placement of troubled teens.

On June 1, Troy kicked another resident in the stomach during an argument over the remote control. Shelter Care forced him out – for good.

The Department of Health and Social Services pressed my mother to ask my father to take Troy because "Troy has found it difficult to accept directions and limitations from his mother and has attempted to put himself in equal states with her."

Succumbing to the pressure, my mother tried to convince my father to take Troy. Recently remarried with a house full of stepchildren in a neighboring city, our father didn't want to rock the boat by having delinquent Troy live with him. Dad took Troy for a few weeks, and then returned him. Dad didn't want to deal with Troy's anger, and Troy wanted to be back with Mom.

Before Troy was born, when our parents lived in Chicago with only Hope and me, Dad advised Mom against her strict disciplinarian techniques. He warned that if she didn't follow his more laid-back parenting approach at *that* time, he wasn't going to come to her rescue later. And he didn't.

Mom's relief having her miracle baby back home was apparent in her smile, and by the Neil Diamond songs she hummed. Making up for lost time, she bought Troy an electric guitar the minute he asked for one, and she treated herself to earplugs.

To save gas money, Mom bought a moped to ride to work; Troy wanted it. She declared he could only ride it with her permission. Instead he took it whenever he wished.

Though she was nine inches shorter than Troy, she once tried unsuccessfully to wrestle the bike out of his grasp. When Chip intervened, Troy unleashed all his rage onto him, beating his face until it was bloody. Mom jumped on Troy's back, attempting to pull him off of Chip. She was little more than an annoyance to the teen volcano. Furious about what Troy did to Chip, she called the police to teach him a lesson.

Troy admitted to a petition charging him with two counts of battery.

The authorities did not have a place to house or rehabilitate Troy. They merely threatened him with "supervision" for one year, and suggested our mother call in to authorities regularly. Troy had nowhere to go, but Mom's house.

Mom told Hope later that what bothered her most was that Troy did not appear remorseful.

Troy's verbal abuse of Mom intensified. Mom did not tell me. She didn't want to worry me; she figured I had enough to worry about being in Hollywood and going on auditions.

Her only defense against Troy's profanity was her look of disapproval. Seeing her haunted eyes lowered broke my heart, and usually made me alter my behavior according to her wishes. Even as an adult, I was affected by that look when she visited my Hollywood apartment. It was this look that stopped me from putting my shoe-clad feet up on my own beanbag chairs.

This look, however, only worked on a conscience capable of guilt. Maybe Troy built up immunity to that look, or maybe, as our father was beginning to suspect, he just did not have a conscience.

10

Teenage Batterer

I was back in Wisconsin visiting my family in early April of 1986. My mother tried to act chipper when she invited all the relatives over for Troy's 16th birthday, but Troy seemed detached and kept disappearing into his room to make notes about something. Finally, Troy appeared with our dog Sassy.

My mother met him with her disapproving look, "Everyone's gone and you didn't even say thank you."

Gregg, who was home during spring break and smelling up the house with Polo cologne, suggested that Troy read the book he was then reading – *How To Win Friends And Influence People* – probably recommended by his latest girlfriend's father, a wealthy entrepreneur who had naturally taken a liking to Gregg.

With on-again, off-again Chip spending the night, my mother had a full house – something which made her feel worthwhile.

The following day, excited about a possible acting job, I flew back to Hollywood. Tim Wood had already gotten me one line in *St. Elmo's Fire* (it was cut) and in *Back To The Future* (it was also cut). He had also talked me up to Bill and Lee Bell, the married couple who produced *The Young and the Restless*. They trusted Tim's vision enough to audition me. After my fifth callback on tape for the soap opera, I attended a party with my friend Bruce.

I liked to hang around Bruce because he was so animated and ex-troverted at social gatherings that he took the focus off of my extremely

52

self-conscious self. My manager phoned the party to tell me I had won the part and a three-year contract.

The first person I called was my Grandma DiLetti, who adored the show, but she had no surprise or lilt in her voice, so I don't think she believed me. My mother was ecstatic, but worried. Hope was skeptical. Gregg was jealous. Troy was quiet.

A couple of days later, Troy asked my mother to use her car.

"Why do you need my car?" she asked suspiciously.

"To go to the park."

She thought about letting him go. Troy had just turned 16, though he didn't have his license yet. Mom wondered if it would be less trouble if she just let him take the car for ten minutes.

"Which park?" she asked.

"Hollywood," he said.

At that point, she began hiding her car keys.

The next night while everyone was sleeping, Troy, with California dreams of his own, stole Gregg's wallet and Mom's keys. He picked up his friend Kevin, and freewheeled all the way through Illinois. Drunk on beer and driving in a thunderstorm, Troy skidded into a tree. The car was totaled but Troy and Kevin, both unhurt, managed to abandon the vehicle.

In days, they were apprehended and put on an armored bus back to Wisconsin, a bus from which they easily escaped. Two weeks later, they were caught, put under juvenile arrest, and bussed back to Wisconsin. Troy was placed in the Racine Detention Facility, half an hour north of Kenosha.

Troy was there for less than a week before he convinced two other juveniles to help him escape by attacking the workers. Four staff members, including three women, were injured in this attempt. Though my mother asked the court to forgive him, the court pressed charges.

For the car and wallet thefts, and escape attempt, Troy was sentenced that June to nine months at Wales, a maximum-security home for juveniles one hour north of Kenosha.

11

The Young And The Restless

1986

I was now Phillip Chancellor III on *The Young and the Restless*. Though I was 24, I had a lot in common with my 17-year-old character. Phillip was sensitive and brooding, having been ignored by his mother and put in boarding school all his life. I pictured my father in the "Why did you desert me?" emotional scenes. Phillip was fought over by the maternal characters of Katharine Chancellor and Jill Abbott, as portrayed by Jeanne Cooper and Jess Walton, both experienced professionals who were extremely supportive to this rookie.

Walking into the CBS Artist's Entrance, I would be handed a pass to pin onto my clothes. After the guard cleared me, I walked the long, white hallway, awestruck at the poster-sized photos of some of the shows that were filmed in this studio over the years: *Let's Make A Deal, I Love Lucy, The Jeffersons, Sonny and Cher, The Carol Burnett Show, The Price Is Right, Capitol*, and *The Young and the Restless*.

At the end of this corridor was a dark stairwell where I would catch my breath, and try to calm my nerves before striding up a flight of steps to the stages. I would've loved shots of Peppermint Schnapps from my bartending days to relax me, but I knew drinking alcohol would get me in trouble if someone smelled it.

My character, Phillip, did not have the will power to resist alcohol. Philip sneaked swigs of booze, became an alcoholic, and would eventually "die" from driving drunk when his shiny red Corvette plunged over a cliff.

My introverted nature was challenged facing the thirty crew members required to watch every scene: make-up, hair, props, wardrobe, lighting, cameras, sound, grips, etc. But I felt "bigger" and "better" each day.

My love interest on the show was the producers' daughter, 16-year-old Lauralee Bell.

Although it might not have appeared so, Lauralee and I were similar. We were both inexperienced and both from Wisconsin, where her family had an estate on picturesque Lake Geneva. I was a working class, closeted, gay guy in his 20s, while she was a naïve, sheltered, teenage, Hollywood heiress. Perhaps we were both in our adolescence, as I was just starting to have fun, since my childhood had been so serious. I made her laugh, especially on the road when we did personal appearances. On the way to our hotel rooms, I would knock on strangers' doors, then race away before they answered. She'd never had a friend who made her sprint on high-heels through hotel hallways. I'd never spent this much time alone with a girl.

A part of me was very attracted to Lauralee, but unlike some other closeted actors, I would not use her for publicity or as an experiment, like I had used Sandy. Besides, I was naturally drawn to men, and I wanted a boyfriend.

I secretly fell in love with the show's florist, Danny Ellis, after he asked me out by leaving an orchid with his phone number attached in my dressing room. Danny had the face of a young Paul Newman.

Very quickly, I understood what my father meant about my mother being smothering, because Danny would allow me no space at all. He gave me an ultimatum in the first few months we were together: if the house I was shopping for wasn't in both our names, he was history. Against my better judgment, I consented to his pressure. Six months later, I fell out of love with Danny and begged him to sign the house back over to me. He resisted, and became very vengeful. Our secret relationship was discovered when I showed up at work one day with a black eye; Danny boasted about giving it to me.

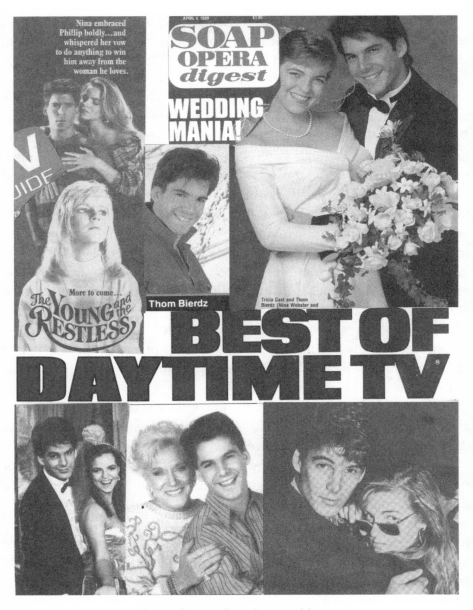

A collage of magazine photos with co-stars
Tricia Cast, Lauralee Bell, and Jeanne Cooper.

12

Juvenile Prison

1987

In January, I returned to freezing Wisconsin, where my mother and I visited Troy. The barbed wire covering the tall chain-link fences made Wales seem like a federal prison even though it only housed troubled teenagers.

Troy met us at an icy picnic table under a dead oak tree. He looked strong and healthy, but his face seemed crooked, asymmetrical.

He stared defensively. My mother sat back, subserviently. She lit a Pall Mall cigarette, and when Troy asked for one, she gave it to him, complaining it was a bad habit.

He told me he watched me on TV, and he got special attention because of my celebrity.

"It's so easy," I said, "the answer to your anger. All you have to do is close your eyes, breathe deep, and visualize a green rectangle the size of a breadbox inside your heart. I learned it in acting class."

He looked at me like I was a stranger. And he was a stranger to me too; this crooked-faced boy, with a cigarette dangling from his lips, sitting across the table from me.

Remembering my adolescence, I said, "I know you're going through the roughest period of your life, Troy. Being a teenager is rough. No one understands."

"I'm not a homo," he declared.

My mother looked up at the winter sky.

I continued, "Close your eyes, breathe deep, visualize...a forest green box inside your heart."

I pointed to my chest. I felt full, complete.

I reached to touch his chest.

"You're fuckin' with me!" he shouted.

"Fuck you then," I said.

"I don't like that word," my mother said, with that look of disappointment on her face.

On the drive home, my mother seemed to be breathing oddly. I figured she was trying to feel the peaceful green forest inside her.

"You should try to feel a hundred evergreens inside your body," I said, "Anyone can, but it helps to close your eyes, so I don't think you should do it driving."

"Will you show me later?"

"Sure," I agreed, feeling grateful that she could see me as an adult now – an adult with his own mind and his own life experiences apart from hers. "I'm learning all kinds of things."

She remarked that she was thrilled I was, but her tone said she was suspicious.

"Mom, it's my life."

"I know. You have a good head on your shoulders. Hard as rock."

I sat with that for a long while, then I whispered, "I got it from you." By the time I finished my sentence, a tear had fallen from her eye to her chin to her hand on the wheel.

She looked at me, "You're my Tommy through and through, you know." Then added, in case I hadn't caught her subtext, "You take after me. Not your father."

I gave her the smile and nod that she expected. I asked about Chip. She explained they still had an on-again, off-again romance.

At her house, I got sidetracked with phone calls and forgot to teach her how to feel the forest inside her. I didn't have time to make sure she gained by my mental exercises. I had my career to take care of. I was a soap star.

Ironically, with every new magazine cover, my world was getting smaller. Soon there was room in it for no one, but me. Though Mom, Hope, and even my jealous brothers praised me for my celebrity, my family was of little use to me. My obligatory annual visits to Kenosha became frustrating because they were starting to resemble my weekend personal appearances at malls around the country. Frustrating because as Mom paraded me around her workplace, I didn't feel as special as she, and the crowd, was carrying on that I was. It was embarrassing not knowing if some policeman really wanted my autograph, or if he was taking it because Mom wanted him to. Embarrassing because these hearty, robust Scandinavian Kenoshans who worked with Mom were twice the size of me, and made comments about how much bigger I looked on TV. Mom assured them, "Big things come in small packages."

I wanted to be taller.

I also wanted to be honest that I was gay. I wanted to say, "Big things come in gay packages." Instead I put on an act at every personal appearance, including Kenosha. At malls, I had started to pretend to be one of the straight soap stars. I studied their stage personalities when I traveled with them, and was learning how to act like them – how to stand, how to smile, how to shake hands. I did it in front of Mom and her co-workers too. I thought it was all worth it when I watched her eyes glow. She filled with pride, giving the impression, and maybe even believing, that a single mother *could* raise successful and well-adjusted children.

13

Schizophrenic Is
What Schizophrenic Does

1987

Troy was experiencing depression at Wales. My method acting exercises might've slightly raised his spirits if he would've tried them, but he refused.

When he expressed interest in astrology and numerology, I got his chart from renowned Kate Diamond. But he didn't care what his rising sign was, or if Jupiter was squaring Saturn.

Troy was released in March of 1987. He continued to skip school, so the school board forced my mother to sign him out of school permanently.

Though it was against her better judgment, Mom also consented to Troy taking karate lessons. The instructor convinced my mother the class would serve as an outlet for Troy's aggression. And for a while it seemed to. At least he wasn't air-kicking an inch from her, or Sassy's face, anymore.

Then one morning Troy strutted through the kitchen with a tattoo on his bicep. Under it was cigarette burns. He said they didn't hurt, and that he no longer felt pain.

Further testing his pain threshold that April, Troy sliced his forearms with razor blades. Mom took him to Kenosha Memorial Hospital and pleaded they keep him there. They agreed.

Troy told the psychiatrist that he was increasingly suspicious of people and groups. He admitted to trying all kinds of recreational drugs to combat the paranoia.

"HAUNTS"
(In the collection of John Riggi & David Wendelman)

Psychiatric Evaluation:

MENTAL STATUS: ...{Troy says}...this is his last life; he
has had ten other lives. This life will not be spent making
money and [instead] inflicting pain on himself, trying
to experience every type of pleasure or possible thing
in life, and eventually to either kill himself, or be shot
trying to save someone. He does not expect to live too
much longer. He says the depression gets so bad that he
likes to inflict pain; sometimes he is afraid that this may
lead to suicide. This date he was oriented, he laughed
whenever I referred to his other lives and seemed to
be aware of attitudes, and of abstract thinking. He has
almost a mildly euphoric happy attitude, [laughing]
somewhat inappropriately and motor activity was full
and comfortable.

Other psychological testing indicated "...evidence of early thinking
disorder, depression, probable adolescent schizophrenia..."

• • •

Our mother discovered a book on paranoid schizophrenia as she was
vacuuming crumbs from under Troy's bed. She formed a question then
that wouldn't be answered for nearly a decade: Is my son a schizophrenic,
concerned for his mental balance, or is he using this textbook to manipulate all of us by faking schizophrenia?

The Kenosha Memorial Hospital prescribed an antipsychotic medication called Navane for Troy. He refused to take the pills, claiming they
gave him lockjaw. Heedless to Mom's protests that Troy needed further
psychiatric care, the hospital released him after only four days.

Troy wasn't happy returning to our mother's house; he demanded his
own apartment and expected her to pay for it. When she refused, he began

"accidentally" dropping Sassy. Mom never told me, that soon after this, she found Sassy crippled. I was only told, due to Sassy's advanced age, she had to be put to sleep.

Mom and Troy went to outpatient counseling a few more times. He refused to continue. Showing up alone humiliated Mom, and she withdrew.

Hope got in touch with me weekly, often from her office where she worked as a computer programmer. During one call, she, upset, recounted the previous night. It was a cousin's wedding and there was access to alcohol. 17-year-old Troy got drunk and threatened Mom. Hope was concerned and didn't want them living together, but she did not have space at her apartment for Troy.

I returned to Wisconsin, insisting on taking Troy to California and finding him a job that would encourage a work ethic and his independence. My mother resisted me, and she whispered that she was worried about what could happen to me.

I didn't care. At that point, I wasn't afraid of Troy.

• • •

The pilot's voice announcing that the plane was about to make its descent startled me out of my reverie. The prospect of landing left me feeling hollow, cold, uneasy, afraid, perturbed, angry, claustrophobic, cornered, and overloaded with dread of what was to come. Rod stirred from his nap. Gregg was once again scribbling on his mysterious piece of pink paper.

It was true that I was not afraid of Troy in the slightest when I asked him to move into my house in California, the year before he killed Mom.

But how could I not have been afraid?

I wondered if I had heard, but ignored his petty crimes and threats, or if I was just so involved with myself that I never even heard the threats against my mother.

I did remember a threat he made against me in Hollywood. He said that he'd learned in Tae Kwon Do class how to point his knuckles like a knife, and stab them through my lungs, so he could rip out my heart in six seconds, and show it to me before I died.

Angry with me and pumped with adrenaline, he quickly demonstrated it in the air, very near my chest.

As I remembered this incident on the plane, and felt sick inside, I had no idea I would come into contact with Troy again. And at that time, when utter madness would be present in his eyes, nothing could prevent him from delivering this threat. If he still wanted to kill me, he would have the chance.

I didn't know then that my worst nightmare would, in fact, come true.

In the future, when I least expected it, Troy and I would meet again.

Face to face.

14

Three Bierdz Brothers
In Hollywood

1988

The roof of my sunny Hollywood house was not yet taken over completely by the pretty-and-innocent-looking bougainvillea plant sporting fuchsia blossoms and winding into my front yard palms. My house, a woodsy oasis on Stanley Street, in the quaint Spaulding Square district of Hollywood, seemed to have begun to lean. The white picket fence out front was graying from traffic, and the birds of paradise on my curb went untended, their dead blossoms turning acid brown.

Gregg had moved in with me a few months earlier at the end of 1987, having graduated from college with a Bachelor's degree in Business Administration and a minor in Psychology. After having DJ-ed the college radio show and hosting a fraternity version of *Family Feud*, Gregg wanted to become an actor. The least I could do was introduce him to photographers, agents, managers, and publicists. The most I could do was get him on *Hollywood Squares* with me. Everybody loved Gregg, but I was irritated he offered no help around the house. Still, I gave him my spare bedroom.

Gregg was not thrilled to share a room with Troy. But there simply was no other place for Troy.

That February, soon after arriving in Los Angeles, Troy decided to join the Army, but the military didn't want him because of his criminal record. In spite of his past delinquencies, I managed to get him a security job. Troy proudly put on the uniform, asked to borrow Gregg's Polo cologne, then posed for a picture we would send Mom as proof of his transformation. But Troy never reported for duty. I didn't know why. I assumed he was lazy and irresponsible, but later I would surmise that paranoia inhibited him. Determined he was not going to just lie around my house all day, I demanded he at least do yard work.

Troy in his security uniform

Troy (left) and me in my L.A. doorway (1988)

I was too busy at CBS to do all the fix-ups an old house required, and my lover Rod was a busy salesman.

Rod did not seem trustworthy to my brothers, but I'd fallen head-over-heels in love the instant we met in a West Hollywood grocery store. I suspect he knew I was on TV before I told him, because I later discovered his ex had also been on a TV series.

Rod asked to move into my home immediately, and I let him. I learned years later that he didn't have a place to live because his ex was throwing him out for cheating. He decided very early in his troubled upbringing to only look at people's mouths, and not their eyes, when they spoke. That way he believed he could tell if they were lying. I was passionate about Rod. He was a genius; a certified Mensa member who could write music with a speed and talent I thought impossible. Sweat would pour from his forehead, as he sat frozen on a bench for hours, mastering various instrument sounds on his synthesizer. My brothers and I were in awe of his talents.

I encouraged Troy to play music and even bought him an acoustic guitar. He fiddled with it for a few weeks, and because of it, he was actually starting to smile and relax. He hummed a few lyrics of Mom's classic Neil Diamond songs when he helped me build furniture. With my friend Bruce's help, we made Adirondack chairs for the back yard. Nothing made Troy laugh like Bruce acting silly or girly. But when Bruce was not around, I was surprised to discover Troy still had a good sense of humor – dry, like mine.

One week, Troy helped me make a giant bed frame out of vertical wooden slats that unwittingly resembled prison bars. I told Troy he was an excellent carpenter, and suggested he get an apprenticeship somewhere. But he didn't want to leave the house.

I tried to get him to do other artistic projects with me.

I loved everything about art: buying oil and acrylic paints, thinning or thickening them, mixing pigments, creating colors, and building up textures. The idea of creating three-dimensions out of a flat two-dimensional

"MICHIGAN TREE MANSION"

canvas was spellbinding, as was learning by trial and error about vanishing points and underlining geometry, and atmospheric perspective like da Vinci utilized in the *Mona Lisa*, where the atmosphere's effect is seen in the representation of distant objects.

Impressed with the shimmering immediacy projected from the landscape oils of Monet and Renoir, I experimented with sunlight and impressionism, but loved that in a stroke of pigment I could change the subtle, sinuous landscape into something more sensuous, or with a bold stroke of color something erotic – and with more strokes from a specialty brush something asymmetrical, like a pre-modern Picasso piece. I would lose track of time, immersed for hours into a canvas, completely trusting my brush as the painting emerged into something from my subconscious.

Even the process of hunting down frames in thrift shops gave me the excited stomach most people get from roller coasters.

I hoped Troy would take an interest, and with training maybe find some career in the arts. But he wasn't interested.

Rod shared tales of his many travels with Troy, hoping to excite Troy with a potential career in some aspect of the travel industry. To no avail.

Rod had traveled the Amazon and was familiar with Rhesus monkeys. We ordered one from Monkeys Unlimited in Cincinnati, Ohio. Fifteen-hundred-dollars seemed like a steal for a primate who could have the intelligence of a four-year-old child. Rod went to the airport with me to pick up Abu, and he bonded more quickly with the terrified pet. To my chagrin, I learned some Rhesus monkeys only bond with one person. Unfortunately for me, Abu chose Rod.

They became remarkably devoted. Abu would sit on Rod's shoulder and instinctively search for bugs in Rod's hair and beard. Rod returned this affection by mimicking Abu and pretending to groom his monkey hair. Then Abu would purr and lower his eyelids in complete satisfaction. I fantasized about Abu looking for bugs in my hair. But much like a colicky baby, he usually screamed when I approached. It was a nonstop, shrill shriek, and the panic in his screams bothered me more than the decibel level.

Having four men and a monkey living under the same roof was often chaotic, often noisy, but just as often silent. Gregg was usually gone – dating or networking or both. Troy preferred to watch TV in his room. Rod and I loved to challenge our word knowledge by playing Scrabble.

Diapered Abu would sit on Rod's shoulder preening his hair, as Rod spent minutes staring at his wooden letter pieces, trying to come up with seven-letter words. I was incensed that Rod could beat me so easily, and I accused him of needing to win everything. Rod argued that I was the one who needed to win everything. I regretted telling him about my grade school dairy questionnaire.

He said, "The rest of the kids hated you for having to outscore them on a stupid dairy test. It was a subconscious effort of yours to get them to keep their distance. Then they couldn't figure out your secret of being gay. Because that was not perfect. You were the lonely schoolboy who lied about his breakfast to impress people. Isn't it weird, or ironic, that you grew up to be a perfect-looking soap opera hunk still lying to impress his fans in shopping malls?"

"I don't lie."

"Thom, I've been there at the personal appearances when the girls ask, 'Do you have a girlfriend?'"

"I said no. I wasn't lying. I was throwing them off. You know that no casting director will cast an openly gay actor. There are no gay songs on the radio. No gay shows on TV. You know what my publicist said..."

Soap Opera Digest had contacted my publicist after a jealous old friend attempted to "out" me, and potentially get me fired from *The Young and the Restless*, by sending the magazine my old pay stubs from the Milwaukee gay bars. Luckily, the magazine, with a reputation of integrity, was happy to disregard them.

Rod asked, "At the malls, didn't you tell them you had a girlfriend?"

"No, that would be lying. I told them I was single, and they cheered that."

"But that was a lie."

If I'd felt more secure about myself, and more secure about my relationship with Rod, I could have fought back. I could have reminded him how he lied every day at his job selling memberships for a heterosexual dating service. Rod regularly told prospective clients he was straight, and that he'd met his true love through the service.

Wasn't that a lie, too?

Was our whole relationship made up of lies?

I was certainly lying as much as he was. When *Soap Opera Digest* did its first cover story on me, I avoided pronouns when asked about a love relationship. It was hard in the beginning to suggest a lie by avoidance, but it got easier. My managers and agents also advised me to "be discreet."

When I took Troy to the set, he wanted me to be discreet too. He was even more embarrassed about my sexuality than I was. Gregg was also embarrassed, but not too ashamed to accept my free room and acting connections.

At my house, however, with the help of Bruce's quick wit and cartoon gestures, my being gay was something my brothers and I joked about. No offense taken. I wanted us to talk about it. So we could get past it.

My brothers and I lifted weights in my garage. Since it was too small for my pick-up truck, we transformed it into a gym with a mirror and a Solo-Flex machine. Even though Troy was the youngest, he had the most muscular definition. Gregg didn't seem to care what we thought about his body; he was only interested in what the ladies thought. The ladies loved his slighter frame with muscular legs from his sports-play. But I was jealous of Troy's physique. He looked more like a soap opera hunk than I did.

But I didn't kick Troy out because I was jealous of him. I eventually kicked him out after he disobeyed me too many times.

Troy's final disrespectful act was to urinate on my front porch. Gregg was using the house's only bathroom, and if Troy couldn't wait he could've peed in the bushes. Instead he chose my front door, and I did not have a sense of humor about that. So I locked him out.

That night Gregg told our mother what happened. She swiftly flew to Los Angeles to rescue and take back home her "miracle baby." At the last minute, I offered to get Troy his own apartment in Hollywood, but she insisted on taking him with her. Surprisingly, after being apart from her for six months, Troy treated her with respect.

They acted loving and appreciative with each other. No one, least of all me, knew the full extent of their dramatic past, or their future. I still did not understand he was a real threat.

Out of sight, out of mind.

I was pleased to not have to put any more energy into helping Troy, and Gregg was grateful to have his own room back.

Troy had only been back in Kenosha for a week before he sent me a diagram of his intended revenge on me. It was a sketch of a man hung from ceiling rafters and hooked up to electrical cables. I dismissed it as an empty threat – another ploy for attention.

But apparently it was more than that. My mother knew it was. That's why she kept her car keys hidden from Troy.

Infuriated that he could not use her car, he grabbed a butcher knife from the kitchen counter, and stated he "would kill everybody and himself" – then slashed his wrist.

He was still bleeding as the police department arrived. Eventually they got him to trade the knife for a pack of cigarettes.

Troy confessed to ingesting a gram of cocaine the previous day. After being examined at the psychiatric hospital, which would not admit Troy because of his history of aggressive behavior, it was determined he had a "conduct disorder or antisocial personality."

The doctor wrote, "I believe this young man requires relatively long-term, highly-structured treatment. I believe that if Troy is not treated at this time, he will soon be untreatable and end up in and out of jail and the court system for various crimes for most of the remainder of his life."

During this time, I was asked to use my celebrity as part of a U.C.L.A. telethon for mentally challenged children. Concerned about Troy, I referred to the kids as "troubled," and was corrected on-air. I couldn't stop thinking about Troy and, succumbing to tears, I shared on camera he had attempted suicide.

For someone like me, who thought he knew everything, who at least seemed to find "success," it was frustrating not knowing how to fix my little brother. The fact that I did seem to fix him, for a couple months, and that I stopped fixing him because of my "Italian temper" and kicked him out, increased my frustration.

15

Troy Chases Love

RHONDA
I see visions of you
through my eyes,
Reminding me of the
Brightest skys.
The times we use to
Walk along remind me
Of a song.
The song begines...
Yet, never ends...
— TROY BIERDZ

1988

In Kenosha, Troy's friend Kevin introduced him to Rhonda Lister. Troy dated her for a few months before she moved hundreds of miles north to River Falls, Wisconsin.

Troy apparently took this relationship more seriously than Rhonda did. After he found out that she quickly acquired a new upstate boyfriend, Troy told Kevin it was time to pay her a visit. On a rainy summer day, Troy and Kevin stole my mother's car and sped north.

In the parking lot of a bowling alley, just outside of River Falls, they chugged beer. A while later they pulled up to an empty police car. It was unlocked. Laughing, Troy reached in and stole the radar detector.

They needed gas and hoped to fill the car and leave without paying. When the clerk insisted they pay first, Troy decided to steal the money by breaking into a soda machine. The police caught them, and they were arrested for possession of the radar detector.

Troy never saw Rhonda again. He was temporarily placed in a holding cell, but when he tried to cut his wrist he was transferred to another psychiatric hospital in Kenosha.

Karen K. Cesenhofer, MSW
Director, Community Support Program

Therapist's Notes:

Troy expressed a great deal of anger toward his mother. He stated he thinks constantly of killing people. He described his thoughts of walking down the street, shooting a stranger and walking on like nothing's happened. He stated he would like to experience the excitement of killing someone.

Troy also reported that he thinks about killing his family, but he cannot do that until he decides whether to kill his mother first or last. He described at length the pros and cons of having his mother watch the rest of the family die or for her to know she would be killed without being able to help the family.

...I encouraged Dr. Carbian to notify the family of what appears to be a potentially dangerous and serious threat to the family in general, but Mrs. Bierdz and brother, Thom, in particular.

Despite the psychiatric evaluation warnings, the hospital discharged Troy after he burned a fellow patient's lip with a cigarette. They released him into the care of our mother, knowing she was at risk.

A few weeks later, Mom wrote a plea for help.

1988 Police Statement By Phyllis Bierdz:

On Friday, September 23rd, in the late afternoon, Troy told me he wanted to go bow and arrow hunting with a friend. He has never gone hunting before. Because I was afraid he would go to River Falls where he has harassed a former girlfriend's family, I said "no." He told me, "I want to kill something. I would enjoy killing something." Later that night, I noticed a large butcher knife in his room. He told me, "I'm gonna need it." The knife has an 8" blade.

On Thursday, September 29th, I had the day off. I was out doing errands. When I came home, Troy told me not to go into his bedroom and I noticed that his door was shut. Later, I went into the room and he had taken some concrete blocks and made a shelf with a board. On the shelf, he had several candles and a globe set out. He had a wicker basket filled with potpourri on the shelf. He had removed everything off the walls of the room and hung up an upside down cross and drawings he had made of devil signs. I made him take the upside down cross down from the wall.

On Friday, September 30th, at about 8:45 PM I was getting ready for work and standing in front of the dresser in my bedroom. Troy came up behind me and took a sock and put it around my neck. He kept pulling it tighter and tighter saying things about how small my neck is and how it wouldn't take much to snap it. I looked into the mirror and could see a terrible look in his eyes and I was very frightened. He kept saying things about my neck and breaking it. This lasted at least a minute. I was afraid and felt a sense of urgency, since he could easily snap my neck, but I couldn't let Troy know how scared I was. I think he would lose perspective and hurt me if he knew how much he was frightening me and I can't protect myself. So, I tried to keep things toned down.

About a month ago, Troy began to get worse and dozens of times he has said to me, "Don't get me mad, Mom. You know what I can do." He has also started taking Karate kicks at my head, just inches from my face. He doesn't say anything, just kicks. He works out all the time and he has had Karate lessons in the past.

On Thursday, October 6th, I came home about 4:20 PM and Troy came into the kitchen while I put away groceries. He told me he didn't want to eat, but then began complaining about losing weight and muscle and how out of shape he is. He hasn't been eating properly lately. He kept watching me and was pacing around. I had the impression he was waiting for something or someone. He tried to help me a little when I hung up a blind. He was complaining about how he was stinking, going on about it for awhile. He finally went to change his underwear, although I couldn't smell anything. He was agitated and pacing around and making phone calls from the kitchen. I had the impression that something he had planned wasn't going to happen and he seemed to become more upset.

At one point while he was on the phone he grabbed me by the shoulder and said, "Don't rile me. You know what I can do; don't make me hurt you." This scared me because he is very strong. He then went into his bedroom and took out a briefcase. Inside there was a case with sharp instruments inside. They were silver. He said something about "cutting instruments". He packed a suitcase very quickly, I think with clothes. His voice was very high and he kept saying something about being at his peak. I bent down and found the cross he had hung on the wall last week and his Spuds MacKenzie doll stuffed under the shelf he had made. The Spuds doll had a vest on and the vest was cut open and Troy said that was an animal sacrifice.

At about 7:10 PM I called the Kenosha police dispatch to notify them that there could be some problems with Troy. I did this because I felt that something was very wrong. Troy kept going in and out of the house each time saying he would be back in ten minutes. He left the house once more and I knew I had to get help. I ran to my bedroom to phone the police, but the cord was cut. This was about fifteen or twenty minutes after my call to the dispatch. I ran to the back door, but couldn't get it open. I ran to the front door, but couldn't get out that way, either. I then saw Troy drive away in my car. I finally got out of the back door and went to the neighbors to call the police. The doors to the house had been tied shut and I found handwritten notes by Troy in the briefcase in his bedroom. These I gave to the police. I could not find the sharp instruments. About six hours later, Troy was found and taken to the hospital for cuts he had made to his arm. I went over to the hospital and when I got my car back I found a number of items Troy had taken with him last night. They were all packed in a blue backpack and placed in the car.

- wedding band and diamond engagement ring belonging to me
- one 2" paint brush
- one metal pulley, 4 1/2" x 2 1/2"
- fifteen metal screws, 2 1/2"
- one nutcracker
- two metal skewers, 18" long
- one can insect repellent

- one screwdriver
- one pair scissors
- one plastic syringe of liquid steel, 11.8 mg
- two small hand saws with hacksaw blades
- one 7 1/2" saw blade
- one 3" saw blade with 8" handle
- one 40" shoelace
- one 12" wooden handle
- one dissecting kit containing probe, scissors, tweezers, pointed metal probe with an empty space for another instrument
Signed by Phyllis Bierdz 10/07/88

Mom was terrified for my safety, as the objects Troy listed matched his diagram of torture for me.

As I sat next to Rod and Gregg waiting for the plane to land, Troy's threat repeated in my mind a hundred times.

Dean Carbian, ACSW Clinical Coordinator Community Support Program

Troy...described how he would kill Thom slowly over about four days, torturing him. He stated he would hang him from his hands, burn him with cigarettes, pound nails into his kneecaps, use a car battery to give him electrical shocks...

Four days.
Torturing me.
Four days. Torturing *me*.
Was Troy waiting, watching our landing?

"ANGER"

16

God Is Dead

1988

T ravelers slowly unloaded from the plane, and since we were
seated in the rear, we had a few more minutes to wait. And
sweat.

I watched Gregg look down into his cupped, flexed hands. Nothing
was there. I couldn't tell if he was almost praying, or almost strangling
Troy.

Was Troy outside waiting for us?

Was Troy totally crazed?

After the police ignored Mom's written plea for help, she managed
to convince Troy to commit himself to Kenosha Memorial Hospital's psychiatric ward in October 1988. He was medicated for six days. His mood
went from euphoric to paranoid, and back again. Troy was suffering the
influence of these mood swings when his friend Michael visited with his
14-year-old brother Steve. Michael's police report repeated in my head,
over and over: "Troy was in the lounge area, Troy was telling my brother
Steve how he (Troy) was going to break out of the hospital and kill his
brother the actor."

Was Troy's real motivation to kill me because of my "fame," and not
that I had kicked him out of Los Angeles?

Was Troy now waiting for us to descend from the plane – and did he
intend to only kill me because I was "famous?" Would he kill Rod and
Gregg too? If he did kill them, was it because a multiple murder would
make Troy more "famous?" As we sat on the plane, we heard disturbing

news about young actress Rebecca Schaefer from the TV show *My Sister Sam*. That very day, she was murdered on her Hollywood doorstep by a schizophrenic fan.

Was this why I was starting, at least subconsciously, to regret the fame I had achieved? Was this partially the reason my fame would soon disappear? Did I hold my fame partly accountable for my brother's jealous agenda to kill and empower himself? Would Troy want to kill me if I were not "famous?"

But Troy didn't want to kill Mom with the sole intent to be "famous."

Why did Troy want to kill Mom? Was it because they were co-dependent? Was it because he hated her personally? Or was it what she represented? And what did she represent?

. . .

At the Kenosha Psychiatric Hospital where Mom had taken Troy, he choked a nurse who looked like Mom, but stopped short of actually killing her. He fought off three more staff members, and then escaped. His whereabouts were unknown for nine days. This is when I was warned for my safety by his psychiatrist. But Troy did not kill me then, show up at my home, or even phone me.

Troy called our mother instead. Lovingly, she manipulated him into returning for psychiatric evaluation. He was kept in leather restraints and screamed his resistance to them, battling the haunted voices in his head.

I believe Troy intentionally revealed different parts of his personality to different doctors over the years. Most diagnosed him as merely antisocial. Some warned of danger and schizophrenia. Others believed he was faking.

As long as Troy kept them all guessing, he remained in control.

A few more doctors examined Troy on the state's behalf, to help with his sentencing in the River Falls incident. They also disagreed on his diagnosis. One believed Troy was mentally sick; the other insisted Troy was faking everything.

The court said that if Troy believed himself to be mentally ill, he could avoid a prison sentence and voluntarily commit himself.

He did.

. . .

Refused by all the Kenosha psychiatric hospitals, Troy was admitted to one in Racine. He was removed for threatening the staff, and put into a holding cell at the Kenosha Safety Building, the jailhouse where our mother worked.

At home, Mom paged through the book on paranoid schizophrenia that Troy kept in his room, sick to her stomach and terrified, unsure if he was faking or not.

Mom confided in others, but not me, about this book, just like she never told me the full extent of Troy's menacing and abusive behavior toward her. I suppose in her mind she was protecting me. During this difficult time, Mom did confess to me that she was beginning to doubt if her prayers were heard. Since Troy's birth, she certainly had little proof God was listening. My soap stardom proved to me that prayers were answered, and I was not troubled when Mom, or friends, shared personal misgivings about the existence of a god. My faith had not been shaken – yet.

. . .

As Rod, Gregg, and I prepared to leave the airplane, our last guaranteed safe haven for who knew how long, I couldn't stop picturing my mother holding Troy's schizophrenia book, kneeling by her bed in front of her ceramic statue of The Virgin Mary, praying, *"Hail Mary, full of grace, the Lord is with Thee. Blessed art Thou amongst women and blessed is Thy fruit of Thy womb."*

How many times did she say that prayer?

When did she realize The Virgin Mary wasn't listening to Phyllis Bierdz?

What evidence did she have The Virgin Mary ever listened to her?

What evidence did she have there was even a God looking out for her?

It certainly seemed unlikely.

God no longer cared.

God was dead.

. . .

On December 22, Mom went shopping for Christmas presents with Hope and Grandma DiLetti. When she returned home, she learned Troy had tried to kill himself by slicing open his wrist in the holding cell.

The next day, he tried to hang himself with bed sheets.

The day after that, he swallowed a spoon, and had to be taken to the hospital to have it removed. He attempted suicide a total of six times until he was harnessed into a straitjacket, yelling profanity at the top of his lungs.

The police tried to have Troy removed from his holding cell to an institution, but because of his history of harassing hospital attendants, no psychiatrist in Kenosha or Racine would admit him back into a hospital.

Throughout that winter and spring, Mom raced around, desperate to find a place that would help Troy.

"CORNERED MOTHER"
(Homage to Matisse)

17

The Last Visit

1989

The flight attendant stopped me before I exited the plane. She said she was sad that I was dead. She had watched my character on *The Young and the Restless* die just a month before in June.

I explained to her the TV aired episodes which we taped several weeks in advance, and that I had actually left when my three-year contract expired in May.

• • •

Rod backed my decision to leave the soap opera and audition for feature films, but family members, especially my parents, were nervous I was giving up my once-in-a-lifetime opportunity.

Though I was very attached to many of the actors on the show – as attached as someone hiding his sexuality could be – I left without saying goodbye to them. It was my pattern to disappear quietly, just like the way I'd skipped my high school graduation.

Another actress on the show, who was not in my storyline, and whom I seldom saw, was also leaving that day. Neither of us showed up on Stage 33, following the last shot of the day, for the farewell party given in our honor. I later learned the producers made a special trip to the stage to present gold watches to this actress and me. They waited half an hour for us to appear before they, confused, ate the cake and went home to their families. I don't know why the actress did not show up, but I didn't show up because I dreaded everyone looking at me all at once, expecting a speech.

What would I say?

Or more importantly, what did they want me to say?

My friend Bruce once made the mistake of throwing me a surprise party. A deer-caught-in-the-headlights look would not leave my face. My panic made the guests uncomfortable and, to my relief, they departed quickly. So, instead of subjecting the cast, the crew, and myself to a similar experience, I opted to end my three years on *Y&R* by sneaking out of CBS's back exit.

A few weeks later in June, just a month before I gave the flight attendant my autograph then exited the plane returning me home for my mother's funeral, Rod, Abu, and I took a cross-country road trip to Wisconsin.

Mom had gone though all her leads on establishments to rehabilitate Troy in Kenosha, Racine, and half of the prospects in Milwaukee before she found what she hoped was a "safe" place for Troy – the Exlogry House. When Rod and I visited Troy in the big city that smelled like breweries, we found no indication he was suicidal at that time in the least. No one else was evident in the structure where he was residing, which looked like a dilapidated house. We questioned the existence of the chaperones that Mom was promised would monitor Troy. If Exlogry House had rules, Troy appeared to be free to violate them daily.

Troy showed us a painting he'd done with the brushes I'd sent him – red figures holding weapons.

We took Troy to lunch. He stared at me over the table, trying to be intimidating. But I wasn't intimidated. I didn't ask him about the diagrams of torture he sent me. I'd never given those a second thought. In his eyes, I only saw a vulnerable, lost boy.

I suggested he save money and move out to L.A. again. He was very quiet.

Later that week, Rod, Abu, Gregg, and I, along with Hope and her husband Sam, and all the DiLetti relatives celebrated my grandparents'

50th wedding anniversary. Troy also attended; dressed in a suit jacket our mother bought him for the occasion. There was evident love between them.

Maybe the time apart was improving their relationship?

Me, Gregg, and Troy at our grandparent's 50th anniversary
party a month before Mom's murder

. . .

The next day as Rod and I loaded the van for California, Mom held onto me, refusing to let me go. She was sobbing.

I thought I understood what she was thinking, so I smiled at her concern, looked into her sepia-brown eyes, and reassured her, "You probably think I'll be hurt in some car accident, but we'll drive carefully. I promise! Mom, stop crying! You're going to see me again!"

But I couldn't pry her off of me.

It was like she knew she would never see me again.

By the time Rod and I were back in Hollywood on July 6, Troy went to court for his previous charges of assaulting hospital personnel, stealing my mother's car, and taking the police radar detector. Troy pled "no contest" and received a four-year sentence.

Amazingly, this could have been exactly what my mother wanted. At last, an institution would be forced to house Troy, treat him, and try to rehabilitate him!

Mistakenly, the court thought it best that Troy serve the first year of his sentence at the Exlogry House, a place with no supervision or rehabilitation!

What would it take to get Troy the treatment he needed?!

My aunt later told me how pale and unhappy my mother looked in that courtroom. Mom readjusted Troy's tie, and asked him to come down the following week from the Exlogry House, with the supervisor's permission of course.

On July 14, he did visit.

He brought along his baseball bat.

18

Arriving In Wisconsin
For Mom's Funeral

July 18, 1989

Leaving the plane steps and entering the terminal of Milwaukee's Mitchell Field Airport, Gregg, Rod, and I were thinking about, but not discussing, the rumors we had heard about how Troy would kill the rest of the family. One rumor said he was seen back in Kenosha buying ammunition, and he told a friend he would stand in the church parking lot, fire bullets at us through the stained glass windows, then drive away. One rumor said he would stab us in our sleep at Hope's house. Another rumor said he was going to force us, at gunpoint, to kill each other.

Afraid of Troy's ambush, we walked close together and attempted to blend into the noisy crowd of travelers. Thankfully, Troy was nowhere in sight. A tall guy in a dark suit approached and introduced himself. We were relieved he was the bodyguard my California friend arranged. The bodyguard suggested he stand near us, but appear like a stranger, not talking to us.

At baggage claim we got Abu, and I released him from his cage. Surprisingly, our beautiful little monkey hugged me. I'm certain he would have hugged anyone after six hours in a freezing, oxygen-depleted, pitch-black chamber full of howling dogs. Abu soon came to his monkey senses and reached for Rod. Rejected, I called Hope to tell her we'd landed.

My father answered.

Hope probably blamed our father for the murder because he left our mother and didn't help raise Troy. Hope would never directly accuse him of negligence. She was anything but confrontational, and rarely said what she was feeling. She would express very little with her soft soprano voice, yet her betrayed doll eyes, like our mother's, spoke volumes.

My father's low, bashful voice trembled with guilt over the phone when he told me that Grandma DiLetti accused him of "ruining" all of our lives when he left Phyllis. My silence didn't confirm, or deny, Grandma DiLetti's remark.

After we arrived in Kenosha, the family gathered at the home of my Aunt Dianne, Mom's sister. A cousin showed me the *Kenosha News*. Troy was still listed as missing. Apparently, one witness saw Troy back in Kenosha, but another said he was near the border of Mexico. We would later learn Troy, who loved the TV show *America's Most Wanted,* was playing phone tag with the Kenosha Police Department. He would call, high on adrenaline, and taunt them.

Over the past days, Troy had been discussed on the evening news in Kenosha, Racine, Milwaukee, and Chicago. But this wasn't just local news anymore. Our family tragedy would soon be plastered on the covers of *The National Enquirer, The Globe, The Star*, and *True Detective.*

My bodyguard agreed to stand watch outside Hope's house that night, in case Troy planned to attack us while we slept. Gregg told the bodyguard to fire at anything that made a noise in the dark.

Gregg was assigned the basement couch, while Rod, Abu, and I, took the ones in the living room. In these unsettling, dark rooms we all lay awake, terrified. I needed my asthma inhaler.

"Shhh," Rod whispered to me, "I think I hear something."

Since we lived close to Sunset Boulevard in Hollywood, we'd forgotten how eerie Wisconsin silence could be.

We heard definite footsteps close to the window. I crept to the door to look out. It was only the bodyguard. But my sister's house had a large backyard with many trees, so Troy could feasibly sneak in through any of the back windows and kill her.

"Do you think Troy has been able to sleep?" I asked.

"I don't know."

"I wonder if he's sorry. He has to be sorry. He had to be sorry immediately, don't you think? As soon as he saw what he did?"

"I don't know."

"She was in the kitchen," I said.

"Shhh."

"Do you think he's killing strangers now?" I asked, catching my breath.

"I don't know."

"Thanks for coming here."

"What else could I do?" Rod said.

"He probably won't kill you. Just me. I'm famous."

When I eventually fell asleep I dreamt of being on an island, a paradise with thick rain. I knew Mom was behind the clouds, but I wouldn't be able to see her until it stopped raining.

It never stopped raining.

"RAIN DREAM"

19

Guilt

<u>July 19, 1989</u>

In the silence of dawn, I peeked out the window. Squinting from the sun, I saw a hummingbird grace my sister's marigolds. I wondered if my mother could see this. I wondered if my mother, in her short 49 years, saw enough marigolds, her favorite flower.

When she walked me to kindergarten holding my hand, we passed lawns with marigolds. Why didn't I ever run over and pick her one? Would she have smiled and thanked me, or given me one of her looks to scold me for taking a flower without permission?

I could have bought Mom flowers with the money I earned as a paperboy. She worked as hard for that money as I did, maybe harder. Each Sunday morning before the sun rose she made me hot chocolate, then lifted the heavy *Milwaukee Journals*, loaded them into her car, and drove me from house to house helping me deliver them. Each wet paper was as heavy as an encyclopedia to me, but my mother, who wasn't much larger than I was, lifted stacks of them. She deserved flowers for helping me, but more importantly, for showing me what someone could accomplish with skinny little arms.

My bodyguard was talking to an African-American officer resembling Ed, a man my mother dated briefly. Ed also never gave Mom marigolds, though once he took her and Troy to the Bahamas. She was trying to be a free spirit then, but the romance didn't last. She never said why.

I opened the window over my sister's couch. The muggy Wisconsin summer air poured into the living room. Either the heat or nerves woke Rod. We went out for breakfast to keep from disturbing the others. I took him to The Ranch Restaurant, and told him my mother had worked there.

Sitting at the counter, Rod and I didn't say much as I thought of the times Mom waited on me there, just like she did at home. I also thought of the times she and I sat together – not at this restaurant counter, but at St. Mark's.

Embarrassed and humiliated, she sat in her "nice clothes" watching the married ladies receive communion. Sometimes I missed the communion call and remained beside her in the pew, so she wouldn't be left sitting alone in the vast sanctuary. Although I'd been raised a Catholic since birth, I couldn't understand why she was denied this most basic ritual. When I finally asked, her eyes darkened and she whispered that she'd gotten a divorce. Her tone, and guilty glances toward the statue of The Virgin Mary, told me she didn't want to discuss it any further.

The treatment my mother received after the divorce may have done more to turn me against Catholicism than did the condemnation I received for being gay. I could choose whether or not to act upon my sexuality, but she had no choice. Mom did not want Dad to leave, and she did not want to get a divorce. How could she be guilty of a sin she did not commit?

I followed my mother's gaze to the Virgin's statue, and wondered if Mary had stopped loving her, as my father had. Did The Virgin Mary also think my mother was too "controlling?"

What would Mary have done if Joseph had left her and her miracle baby?

20

A Damning Funeral

July 20, 1989

Leaving diapered Abu on a long leash tied to the kitchen table, Gregg, Hope, our father, Sam, Rod, the bodyguard, and I drove to the funeral. We unloaded from my sister's van. Walking toward the church that condemned our mother for being divorced, and me for being gay, I wanted to hold Rod's hand, but chickened-out.

The hundreds of stained-glass windows circling the tall chapel reflected the blue of the dozens of police officers in attendance or guarding the various entrances.

We sat in a front pew, my bodyguard on the end. A soft hand from the pew behind brushed my shoulder. It was Aunt Mary, Mom's best friend, confidante, and youngest sister. She was a sensitive beauty, with the smoothest skin and most haunted eyes of all of us – eyes like dark, unending tunnels. She ran her fingers over the rosary around her neck that five days ago hung in my mother's bedroom. I followed Aunt Mary's lingering glance to Grandma DiLetti. In the sanctuary's flickering candlelight, my grandmother's face was so contorted it was barely recognizable. Hearing her wail of sorrow, I understood why her face would be so disfigured from grief. Grandpa DiLetti's, "Shhh, Jenny," had no effect on her.

My grandfather didn't like the sound of crying, or of any noises. Abandoned seventy years earlier in Italy, he had learned early in his life that other people would tolerate his presence, and even feed him, if he kept quiet, worked hard, and caused no trouble. This may have been where our family trait of keeping turmoil inside originated. Grandpa DiLetti was an

"HOUSE OF DRAMA"
(In the collection of Scarlett Johannson)

expert at it. He had barely uttered a word since he discovered his daughter's lifeless body. He remained completely composed, transfixed by her casket.

The large choir sang Mom's favorite hymn, *Let There Be Peace on Earth*. Hope glanced at the door, terrified Troy might suddenly appear. Sam put his arm around her to protect her. In just a few weeks, this ordeal would turn Sam's black hair to gray.

After the hymn, the priest offered prayers for the souls of our mother and Troy. Though he didn't say so directly, he implied that Troy's soul was damned to Hell.

If Troy was damned for killing our mother, was I damned too?

I had also taken a life. As the priest continued to speak, all I could think about was killing my pet guinea pig. I didn't commit murder intentionally, as we were all sure Troy had. Did that make my actions any less heinous, any more forgivable?

My loving pet didn't have a chance.

In an instant he was gone, leaving nothing but dead mass in my hands.

I accepted my guilt, but was I forgiven? My poor pet didn't know I wasn't trying to hurt him. Did *he* forgive me?

In the last moments before her death, did our mother forgive Troy?

For the first time since hearing my mother was dead, my eyes welled with tears. Rod patted my back as the choir sang. The shedding of silent tears wasn't because my mother was gone; my spiritual beliefs, which I clung to like never before, guaranteed she existed somewhere. And I was trying to be happy for her transition.

I cried for myself in St. Marks, probably a long overdue cry, because I still feared damnation. Buried deep within my gentle psyche, I held on to the childhood belief I was going to burn in Hell forever, not just for being gay, but also for accidentally murdering my beloved pet.

I silently cried, also, because I had shamed my angel of a mother.

I cried mostly, though, because a little boy shouldn't have been raised to feel so guilty and damned.

. . .

The choir ended the song. Gregg was called up to give a prepared eulogy. When I figured out this was happening, I was stunned.

I looked at Hope, who whispered, "I hope you don't mind. We decided one of us should say something, and Gregg volunteered."

"What about me?" I whispered.

"But Gregg said he wanted to."

At the altar, Gregg unfolded the piece of pink paper from the airplane, the one he'd been writing on while seated with me. I felt betrayed. I was also jealous – jealous that Gregg trumped my celebrity to speak on our behalf. Jealous that, unlike me, Gregg was confident in being the center of attention. Jealous that Gregg took a moment and locked eyes with our uncles in the pews. I was always too embarrassed to look my uncles in the eyes. Maybe they would see I thought they were handsome – wasn't that a sin?

Gregg frowned sympathetically at our weeping Aunt Dianne, the most sensitive, most supportive, least judgmental person in the family. Finally, staring purposefully at a newspaper reporter, he ended the eulogy with a series of compliments about our mother.

After Gregg spoke, my uncles and cousins carried my mother's coffin through the sea of distorted faces. I followed, overhearing them whisper, "How tragic. Aunt Phyllis is dead."

My thoughts were quite different: From where was my mother looking? Was she floating above us? Was she trying to remember and place all these faces? Did she think she was still alive? Was she pulling on Aunt Mary's rosary, trying to figure out why there was a funeral for her? Was she speaking to all of us? If she was, why couldn't I hear her?

Or was she still with Troy?

And where was Troy?

21

The Fall Of Troy

July 21 to November 16, 1989

On July 21, Troy was arrested for breaking into a car at a mall parking lot in Laredo, Texas, near the Mexican border. With him was the hitchhiker he'd been traveling with for almost a week.

On July 23, both young men were flown back to Kenosha and interviewed by detectives.

Troy, against his defense attorney's advice, admitted his guilt in writing on August 16. The next day his note was printed in the newspaper.

Kenosha News:

I, Troy Alan Bierdz, am competent and would like to plead guilty of the charge of the death of my mother. I, Troy Alan Bierdz, would simply like to walk into court plead guilty and be sentenced the same day. I want a speedy sentence!

Mr. Zielski, Troy's state-appointed attorney, who had previously defended Troy, pleaded with the judge that the confession was invalid, and that Troy was not in his right mind and was therefore incompetent to speak on his own behalf.

The judge demanded a psychological examination to determine Troy's competence.

Dr. Drowley, a forensic psychiatrist who knew nothing of Troy's history, was called in to decide Troy's mental capacity.

William J. Drowley, MD
September 1, 1989, Examination Report:

...My interview with Troy certainly did not produce anything approaching sufficient data for me to make a diagnosis of mental disease. Nevertheless, there were a few hints that this could be the case. One of these hints occurred during the mental status examination when I asked him what way a fly and a tree are alike or similar. His response was an excellent one when he said "living things." Later in the interview, however, he asked me about that particular question, wondering if he had answered it correctly. He then, by way of explanation, said that there are frequently flies around trees, flies are insects, insects are on fruit and this related back to the original question of similarities that I had asked him which was in what way are an orange and a banana the same or similar. He had replied to this question with "fruit." His desire to somehow connect all the questions all together and make some sort of coherent whole out of them and the somewhat circuitous reasoning that he employed suggests the presence of thought disorder...

Despite the above comments, the probability of Troy having a mental disease which would serve as a basis for a special plea is not very great.

I would like to make one final comment. It strikes me that the pivotal issue here is whether or not Troy's present behavior, as reflected in his interview with me, is willful or not. On the surface it certainly appears to be but if he were suffering from a mental disease, and his need to hide that fact precluded a rational assessment of an "insanity" plea then he might be incompetent to stand trial. It might also be that he is presently so guilt-ridden over his act that he is driven to act in a way which will bring maximum punishment onto himself and part of that could be not participating in his defense. This might also render him incompetent to stand trial.

I am not stating that it is my opinion that he is not competent to stand trial, I simply don't know...

On September 22, Zielski tried to get the murder charge dismissed, because the hitchhiker in his first interview said he did not notice if there was blood on Troy's clothes. The motion was denied.

September 26, 1989. Courtroom Transcript:

MR. BRECKER, PROSECUTING ATTORNEY: *Basically, what Dr. Drowley states in his letter to Mr. Zielski is that he doesn't know. And I think he knew that, that he didn't know, prior to even examining Mr. Bierdz that he didn't know. I think if we were to ask any psychiatrist, any doctor or psychologist in the State of Wisconsin, is Mr. Bierdz competent to stand trial? All they could say was the same that Dr. Drowley says – "I don't know."*

THE COURT: *...what strikes me, what troubles me about Dr. Drowley's report, first, I didn't even understand anything particularly curious about Mr. – or Dr. Drowley's report of Mr. Bierdz' conversations of about a fly in a tree. I didn't think there was anything peculiar about what Mr. Bierdz said; nor did I think it was especially relevant to this case. Although Dr. Drowley deals with a lot of thought disorders and it may have been some sort of a red flag to him. What troubles* *me most of all about Dr. Drowley's report is where he says it might also be that he is presently so guilt-ridden by his act that he is driven to act in a way which will bring maximum punishment unto himself, and part of that could be not participating in his defense. This might also render him incompetent to stand trial.*

And I think now we have reached the nadir of the relationship of law with psychiatry. If I interpret that statement correctly, what the physician is saying is that the fact that – if this man is guilty, the fact that he killed his mother with a baseball bat and that he feels guilty as a consequence makes him crazy. That's how I read it. He is saying, as I understand what he is saying here, is if he feels guilt, so guilt-ridden over the fact that he beat his mother to death with a baseball bat, that he wants to go in and admit it and take his punishment, that, therefore, he is crazy. That's very disturbing to me, that the physician would say such a thing...Mr. Bierdz, do you understand what's happening here today?

DEFENDANT: *Yah, I think so.*

THE COURT: *Do you want to try to explain to me in your own words what you understand is happening?*

DEFENDANT: *Um, checking to see if you should send me in for a psychiatric evaluation.*

THE COURT: *Why would I do that?*

DEFENDANT: *Um, to see if I am competent.*

THE COURT: *How do you feel about that?*

DEFENDANT: *I figure the judge's decision is the judge's decision.*

THE COURT: *Do you know what the charge against you is?*

DEFENDANT: *Murder.*

THE COURT: *And do you understand what can happen if you are found guilty of murder?*

DEFENDANT: *Yah.*

THE COURT: *What is that?*

DEFENDANT: *I can be sent to prison.*

THE COURT: *For how long?*

DEFENDANT: *I am not sure of the time.*

THE COURT: *Have you been told that you could be sentenced to prison for the remainder of your life?*

DEFENDANT: *Um, I have been given like–*

THE COURT: *(Interrupting) I didn't hear you.*

DEFENDANT: *I have been given variations in time that I could spend in prison.*

THE COURT: *...Do you – have you had a chance to discuss with Mr. Zielski the plea that you wish to enter in the court?*

DEFENDANT: *Well, yah.*

THE COURT: *...Do you feel you understand what Mr. Zielski is saying to you?*

DEFENDANT: *Yes.*

THE COURT: *Do you have any unresolved questions with him?*

DEFENDANT: *No.*

THE COURT: *Do you feel you have had enough time to confer with him about this case?*

DEFENDANT: *Yah.*

THE COURT: *Are you presently experiencing any physical discomfort in the jail?*

DEFENDANT: *No.*

THE COURT: *Are you hearing any voices from persons you don't see?*

DEFENDANT: *No.*

THE COURT: *Are you having any difficulty with seeing things or hearing things?*

DEFENDANT: *No.*

THE COURT: *Are you having any trouble sleeping?*

DEFENDANT: *No.*

THE COURT: *Have you lost any weight in the jail?*

DEFENDANT: *No.*

THE COURT: *How long have you been in jail now, sir?*

MR. ZIELSKI: *Since July [23rd].*

THE COURT: *Now, do you feel that you want to offer a defense to the Court in respect to this case?*

DEFENDANT: *No.*

THE COURT: *The physician here says that he has some concern that you may be so guilt-ridden over this act, that you are desirous of actually receiving the maximum penalty I can give you. Do you feel that's an accurate statement?*

DEFENDANT: *No, I don't feel that I want–*

THE COURT: *I'm sorry.*

DEFENDANT: *I don't feel that I want to be put away for the rest of my life.*

THE COURT: *Well, if you are convicted of this offense, you understand that will be the sentence?*

DEFENDANT: *Yah.*

THE COURT: *So, in other words, you feel you have something that you want to present in terms of a defense to the case?*

DEFENDANT: *No.*

THE COURT: *You just want to try to get a shorter sentence?*

DEFENDANT: *Yah.*

THE COURT: *Okay. If part of that involved your testifying in the court, do you think you would be able to do that, coming onto the witness stand?*

DEFENDANT: *I would prefer to use the right to remain silent and sit here other than get up on the stand.*

THE COURT: *No. I am not – perhaps my question wasn't clear. If Mr. Zielski thought it was to your advantage to testify, to take the stand in this case and answer questions about this incident surrounding the death of your mother, do you think you would be able to do that?*

DEFENDANT: *Yah.*

THE COURT: *Do you think that you could discuss the case freely with Mr. Zielski?*

DEFENDANT: *Yah.*

THE COURT: *Have you ever been diagnosed as being mentally ill, do you know?*

DEFENDANT: *Yah, I think so.*

THE COURT: *When and where?*

DEFENDANT: *I couldn't tell you.*

MR. ZIELSKI: *I was his attorney, your Honor.*

THE COURT: *You were his attorney?*

MR. ZIELSKI: *Yes.*

THE COURT: *Who judged him mentally ill?*

MR. ZIELSKI: *Judge Breitenbach.*

THE COURT: *He was committed?*

(Mr. Zielski shows Judge Shneider examination reports.)

THE COURT: *Demonstrates paranoid schizophrenia. Alright. Now, you were hospitalized after that, the report by Dr. Chiotola; is that right?*

DEFENDANT: *Um, yah.*

THE COURT: *For how long was that?*

DEFENDANT: *I couldn't say.*

THE COURT: *I'm sorry.*

DEFENDANT: *I don't know...*

THE COURT: *...Have you discussed it with Mr. Bierdz?*

MR. ZIELSKI: *With myself.*

THE COURT: *With Mr. Zielski?*

DEFENDANT: *Well–*

THE COURT: *What?*

DEFENDANT: *He is my attorney. I will tell him what I want to tell him. I have the right to remain [refrain from] any questions that I want. I will give him the information I want and let me do what I want.*

THE COURT: *Let's assume for a minute that you want to plead guilty. And*

I am just assuming. Let's assume you want to plead guilty and you have also told me you don't want to go to prison for a thousand years.

DEFENDANT: *I don't think I could live that long.*

Examination By Dr. Drowley:

Troy's journal suggests the presence of a very serious psychiatric disorder. The theme that pervades his writings is essentially that he is the personification of evil. In this view of himself he goes into compulsive detail about every evil thing that he has done in his life including attempting to enumerate various insects that he has killed. Interspersed in his preoccupation with his badness are references to God and church in which he seems to reflect a desire, seen as realistically hopeless, to be something other than evil...

October 4, 1989. Courtroom Transcript:

MR. ZIELSKI: *Your Honor, first I would like to address – further address the issue of competency which was raised at the last hearing. I have supplied the Court with a copy of a letter from Dr. Drowley, which I believe the Court received yesterday after I received it.*

THE COURT: *Yes, I did get it.*

MR. ZIELSKI: *The District Attorney also.*

MR. BRECKER: *Right.*

MR. ZIELSKI: *That letter is dated September 28th. I'm sorry it took so long to get to the Court. It was delivered to the courthouse instead of my office.*

THE COURT: *I saw it. I don't know where it is now, but I had it and I read it. I must have misplaced it. But I know what it said...*

MR. ZIELSKI: *...for the first time Troy indicated to me that inner forces are guiding his decisions in this matter and that he wishes to be* *evaluated for his competency so that he can be sure he knows what he's doing.*

THE COURT: *He's smirking right here in the court. The record will reflect that.*

The court then appointed Dr. Frederick Hosdal to examine Troy on the issue of his competency to stand trial.

October 7, 1989. Dr. Frederick Hosdal, MD Examination Report:

Understood his attorney had requested this exam – said he had heard my name mentioned in court. Objected to an 'insanity' plea and said that a mental illness plea would be 'an easy way out – it was my mother.' Said he wants to be found competent to stand trial. Understood the terms concurrent and consecutive.

When asked about the present charges he said, 'It's about murder – the end result is I struck my mother with a bat and killed her...she got on my nerves – no issue at all – I just wanted to kill her – she is a woman constantly controlling – she got on my nerves.' (I told him that I was sure it was not that simple.) When asked why he used a baseball bat he said, 'it was the only thing I had at the time.'

When asked about his future disposition, said he wants to plead guilty – does not want to plead mental nonresponsibility – 'I did it – I'll take the maximum term – whatever the judge says.' Says he feels bad about being in jail, but doesn't feel bad about what he did to his mother – 'it's no big deal – she was a bitch.' Said he has not cried about what happened.

As to the issue of his competency to proceed, there

was no evidence of mental impairment such that would
cause him to lack substantial capacity to understand the
charges/proceedings against him, or to be able to assist
in his own defense.

Thank you for this referral, and if you or the attorneys
involved have any further questions, please feel free to
contact me.

Was Troy mentally competent to stand trial? During one hearing,
Zielski stated Troy did question his own competency to stand trial, but
Troy objected to an insanity plea when later interrogated by Dr. Hosdal.
Throughout all the psychiatric examinations in the years leading up to our
mother's murder, Troy always seemed to present each doctor with a different facet of his personality. Consequently, his mental status was never
clearly determined. But I believed Troy controlled these facets and that
the facets were not controlling Troy.

At the time of Troy's hearings, I had no interest in his competency,
or in any aspect of the court proceedings. I did not share the rest of the
family's vendetta against Troy, or their need to see him punished, so I
remained in Los Angeles throughout the trial.

Troy thought he killed our mother, but as far as I was concerned *he*
was the one who was dead.

When court reconvened on October 19, the defense attempted to elic-
it sympathy by presenting a study about boys who committed matricide:

Matricide By Sons, 1981, By Christopher M. Green:

58 male patients who had killed their mothers were
studied. The average IQ was 103. Six of the patients had
personality disorders. The rest were schizophrenic or
depressive.

This study illustrated how single, dominant, and possessive mothers
could create sons dependent upon them. The sons grew hostile and resent-

ful, and they were unable to have healthy emotional relationships with other women. These sons usually killed their mothers in the bathroom or kitchen with a blunt object, when there was a threatened separation of mother and son. The sons did not express remorse, only relief.

Aside from short visits, Troy spent nearly three months isolated at Milwaukee's Exlogry House prior to killing our mother.

Troy's attorney's ploy for a lenient sentence did not evoke any sympathy from the court. The judge gave more credence to the Victim Impact Statements filed by our family on November 14.

Each in their own way, asked for Troy to be locked away for life. Remaining in California, I did not make a statement, but wanting my family to feel safe, I hoped Troy was locked up forever.

AUNT DIANNE: *Because of this I am always afraid for my children. It's like a big hollow pit in my stomach...I am sort of torn because of my love for my sister – I know how much she loved her son and how much she did to keep him out of prison. But prison is where he belongs.*

AUNT MARY: *I feel the judge who allowed him to go into the half-way house should be held accountable. To my knowledge no one followed up on Troy.*

GREGG: *The act is INEXCUSABLE. The only way the offender will ever contribute to society will be behind prison walls. Nothing can change his misbehavior period.*

SAM: *Normal looks from strangers take on new meaning. Wrong calls are more suspicious...You spend countless hours each day wondering what you could have done to prevent what happened.*

HOPE: *I am afraid to be alone at night. I think every wrong number is from Troy or one of his acquaintances...My faith in human nature no longer exists...Troy deserves to die but since we do not have the death sentence he should receive life without parole...I am no longer a whole person. I am a shell void of being able to love and give. There is so much to do to put my life back together – if it can be put back together.*

"OUR BACKYARD IN KENOSHA"

True Crime Magazine:

Wisconsin law would require Judge Shneider to sentence Bierdz to life imprisonment, which ordinarily would mean he must serve 13 years and 9 months before becoming eligible for parole. But under a new statute that went into effect earlier in the year, a judge could require a convicted murderer to serve more time before reaching parole eligibility, in effect making his jail time before parole long enough to keep him behind bars for the rest of his life.

On November 16, 1989, Judge Shneider followed the letter of the law. He sentenced Bierdz to life in prison, adding the provision that he not become eligible even for parole for fifty years. 'If he is willing to kill his mother, it seems a far easier thing to kill a brother or a cousin or a stranger,' he said.

Troy was the first person to be sentenced under Wisconsin's new "Life Meaning Life" statute, and he would not be eligible for parole until he was 69-years-old. Unless Troy escaped, he would probably die in prison. He was already dead to me as a brother and as a human being.

I was sure that our mother's soul lived on without a body – and that Troy's body lived on without a soul.

• • •

Little did I know that in about four years, in a seemingly miraculous chain of events, I would be brought face to face with Mom's "soulless" killer; the person who had threatened many times to rip out my heart in six seconds so he could show it to me before I died.

When that day arrived, Troy would find a new way to rip out my heart.

113

"IN SCREAMING CITY"
(In the collection of Kristopher Trust)

22

Reputations

1990

By March, I had spent eight months declining social invitations because I was, for the first time, reassessing what was important in my life. I wasn't sure a social life was important. I was starting to think maybe family was important.

Gregg, as far as I was concerned, was my only brother, and I wanted us to see more of each other. I even had dreams we could work together on projects in the entertainment industry.

But Gregg always puzzled me. Earlier in the year, he stunned me by giving up his dream of becoming an actor. I might have understood his decision if he experienced the same insecurities and inadequacies I did during auditions, but he never explained his feelings. When I tried to talk him into reconsidering, he would only say that he had his reasons.

Gregg only opened up and confided in me when I joined him, which I did on rare occasions, at one of the trendy bars along Sunset Boulevard. He chose places frequented by the successful entertainment industry types he admired and hoped to impress. Gregg acquired a simple, but cynical, philosophy during his short time in Hollywood: "The only way to make it in life is if you come from a wealthy family or 'know' the right people."

I did not share Gregg's determination to emulate Los Angeles' rich and powerful, but I did crave his ability to be in a crowd without anxiety. One particular night, I had an excellent opportunity to observe his control and social ease. It began when I inadvertently ended up walking directly behind him at a packed bar. From this position I discreetly watched

Gregg "in action." He leaned into the bar and yelled, to be heard over the loud barflies, to the bartender about a sports game, and then asked for two beers, "Make them cold ones." His manner was so familiar I thought Gregg knew the bartender, but he didn't.

As I sipped my beer and followed Gregg through mobs of would-be starlets, I continued studying him. What was it about him that turned people's heads?

In the less crowded garden, which still smelled of too many perfumes, I copied Gregg's sexy walk. He lit up a cigar and gulped down half his beer. I did the same. This was like an exercise in my old method acting class. I was trying to invent a new personality. The bitter smoke taste and the yeasty beer were giving me an inner perspective of who he was.

I mimicked Gregg ogling women. He was never intimidating or objectionable, simply appreciative and very funny. His playful stares and cute innuendos were met with batted eyelashes and, remarkably, salutes from these women's husbands or dates.

Gregg thought nothing of giving his phone number to a cocktail waitress, even if she'd already told him he was too short for her. He would tell her big things came in small packages, and he wouldn't dwell on the insult. But thinking back on the times I had been similarly insulted, I fixated on it, neurotically playing it over and over in my head.

As Gregg circled the bar talking to women, I, pretending to read a band flyer, watched him. A gorgeous girl stopped to talk to him, then walked towards me. I nervously turned away and picked up another flyer.

She took it out of my hands. "Are you really on a soap opera? I can't tell if your brother is serious or not," she smiled.

"Yeah. I used to be on a soap."

She studied me more closely.

"That's right! You were Katharine Chancellor's grandson."

"Phillip."

"Your brother said he'd buy me a beer if I asked you to dance."

I stopped smiling. The silence made us both nervous. I chugged the rest of my beer.

She said, "Can I buy you another beer?"

"Nah. I've had plenty." I looked at her glass. It was empty, but I stopped myself from offering to buy her a drink because I didn't want to lead her on.

"Can I ask you something personal?" she asked.

"Yes," I said, avoiding her eyes, expecting to defend my sexuality.

She said, "I read about your family in the rags. Whose side are you on? Your mother's or your brother that killed her? I read she was strict and tried to put him in jail and all kinds of stuff."

I couldn't believe her misconceptions. "I think you need a lot more information before we continue this conversation," I said. "She was an innocent, very loving mother, and Troy was just...mean."

"It sounded like Troy was a victim of abuse or something. I'm sorry."

"I don't know what you read, but our mother never abused us."

"I'm sorry. It's none of my business, but I'm studying behavioral psychology and–"

"You didn't know my mother."

"I've read about lots of killers and usually they are from abusive homes. I'm sorry. Don't be mad."

"You have a lot of nerve accusing a woman you never met."

I walked away, my head reeling. I told Gregg what had transpired, and he quickly pulled me out of the bar.

I often dwelled on challenging or negative remarks, so as the days passed, these accusations against my mother grew more unsettling to me. How could a stranger criticize my sweet mother and blame her for her own death? *Mom* wasn't on trial.

Trying to convince myself this girl was wrong, I read up on as many cases of matricide as I could. I was very disappointed to discover that many perpetrators were indeed abused by their mothers. But Troy wasn't abused by anybody. Was he? Was there something I hadn't seen, or didn't remember?

23

Menendez Brothers

1990

I reflected on another infamous matricide/patricide – the murders of Jose and Kitty Menendez. On August 20, 1989, a month after Troy killed our mother, Eric and Lyle Menendez killed their parents in Beverly Hills. In the ensuing media circus, the young men portrayed themselves as abuse victims. Their defense lawyers tried to convince the juries that these men had blown their parents to bits in self-defense by citing alleged, and to me unconvincing, incidents of sexual abuse by their father.

Overhearing conversations in the grocery store, I suspected many people held Kitty and Jose Menendez partly responsible for their own vicious murders. To me, this coincidental murder case reflected peripherally on my mother's reputation. As her oldest son, I accepted the challenge to convince the world that my mother was not to blame for her own murder. With this goal, I began writing a screenplay about her life and struggles.

I asked the Kenosha Courthouse if they had any legal documents pertaining to my mother that would help me write my screenplay.

"Oh, you betcha," the woman replied.

"Could you send me some Xeroxes?"

"All of them?"

"Yeah. Please."

She grunted. I incorrectly assumed she was a lazy employee. I never imagined she was pulling up hundreds of pages.

A week later, the package arrived.

It contained four hundred pages of court documents: the total legal history of Troy and my mother, including Troy's teenage writings and diaries.

There's no describing the sinking feeling in one's stomach evoked by seeing an organized chronological record of abuse ending in the murder of their mother. Why hadn't she shared with me everything that was going on – and the degree of Troy's abuse of her? Why hadn't the courts put an end to it? Why wasn't there some intervention program established that could have detoured my brother's reign of terror? Reading through the court records, I tried to locate and understand the source of Troy's murderous rage.

Shockingly, in a few months, I would discover its source in myself, when I would viciously vent my fury on a victim even tinier and more helpless than my mother.

24

Hollywood Pawns

1990

G regg had begun calling me at least once a week, dragging me away from my dark thoughts. From his job as an assistant for a successful acting agent, he'd phone with some random memory about an old neighbor or babysitter from Kenosha, or tease me about my childhood crush on Buddy Klopstein. We shared jokes about those awkward times that no one else in the world would have appreciated. As enmeshed in Hollywood hierarchy as Gregg got, his thoughts still gravitated to his childhood. Those were his happiest times. His high school basketball championships and his college popularity empowered him much more than all his attempts at Hollywood networking did.

During these calls, Gregg would abruptly hang up midsentence if his boss entered the room.

Since Gregg liked showing off his three-way calling feature, he sometimes included our father in our conversations. Dad appreciated our light moods, as it was rare for him to hear me laugh out loud. It was an uncomfortable realization that my mother's death opened up my relationship to my father. I no longer had to keep alive her grudge against him for abandoning us. I had by then "abandoned" Danny and was with Rod. I could empathize with Dad's reasons for leaving Mom. As a grown man, I could start to appreciate my father's positive qualities like his intelligence, kindness, patience, and compassion.

Gregg also appreciated these qualities in Dad, and wished his latest boss, who was our father's age, possessed the same respectful and laid back attitude.

Unfortunately, Gregg began working for a personal manager, a gay man with a horrible reputation as a boss. Horrible if you were an attractive straight man like Gregg.

Gregg told me this man paid up to ten-thousand-dollars to have sex with well-known actors and young Hollywood hopefuls. Gregg was daily dodging this man's sexual advances, and was half-tempted, he said, to accept a blowjob as the offer to him personally was reaching twenty-five-thousand-dollars.

Apparently it was permissible for Gregg and his boss to discuss blowjobs at work, but Gregg said, it would be disastrous if anyone in the business knew about Mom's murder at the hands our psychotic brother. That information would seriously jeopardize his career. And he warned me never to mention a word of it.

Until this time, I had managed to keep the fact I was working on our mother's screenplay a secret. But when I told Gregg some of the disturbing things I was reading in Troy's old diaries, I had to come clean about having the court documents in my possession. When he inquired why I all of a sudden sent for court documents, I had to reveal everything. He flew into a rage at the thought I could air our dirty laundry in a public screenplay.

My relationship with Gregg was never easy, but my need to explore and expose the truth divided us further. From this point on, he became suspicious and guarded around me.

Sorting through more of Troy's court records, I was both fascinated and horrified to discover I was not as unique in the family as I believed myself to be. My brother Troy not only resembled myself physically, he also harbored a whole creative side. Mom had presented many of Troy's drawings, Satanic in nature, to the courts in an effort to get him counseling. Troy was a gifted artist. I had no idea he had done any drawings that didn't include weapons. I was even more stunned to discover his flair for verse; though the subjects he wrote about were shocking and ghoulish, I could not deny his natural talent.

CONFUSION
VOICES I hear, visions I see...
Present, past and soon to be.
— TROY BIERDZ

PARANOID
No one's there, I'm paranoid
Are you sure there's no one there?
But I see them
No one's there
Are you sure no one's there?
They're staring
No one's there
They're laughing
No one's there
Stay in control
No one's there
— TROY BIERDZ

One afternoon I came home from a thrift shop with a huge frame for a portrait of Mom I'd soon attempt. I planned on giving the framed picture to Hope, because even if she hadn't talked about Mom, I assumed she must have been missing her.

Rod snooped through my box of court records at the kitchen table, while Abu affectionately groomed his hair. I reached for Abu and he scowled in fear as he usually did when I got close to him.

The phone rang. It was Sandy, the girl I dated in high school. She'd been trying to locate me since she heard about Mom's murder, but her sympathy quickly turned personal. She wanted to know why I dumped her years ago. I froze, still afraid to tell her I was gay. I simply said, "I don't know." She kept asking if there was something wrong with her. I said no. She cried, saying she was still in love with me. I wanted to hang up, but couldn't hurt her feelings that way, so I listened to her cry for half-an-hour. She finally hung up. I felt ashamed and powerless. I reached for Abu.

When Abu screamed at me in front of company, I ignored it. But I didn't ignore it when we were with Rod. How dare Abu still scream at me, and prefer Rod, after two years! I paid for him *and* loved him *and* fed him *and* tried to play with him *and* built him his extravagant cage. I was not going to allow this monkey to not love me. I grabbed him. He shook loose and ran to the back of the house. I chased him. I would have been the perfect loving parent, if only he'd let me, but he never stopped screaming at me. He hated me. He was terrified of me.

Each time I tiptoed near him, his curdling holler slit my guts. His terrified monkey face bobbed to hide from me. He darted in every conceivable direction to avoid me.

Abu jumped into Rod's comforting arms, enraging me. My fury mixed with the shame I felt about Sandy, and my hidden anger at Rod. Several friends claimed he was being unfaithful to me. Rod denied he was cheating, but I didn't believe him.

Before going out for the evening, Rod carried Abu into the bedroom, and put him in his cage with a banana.

As soon as Rod left, I decided it was time Abu learned to love me. Or else.

"THE PROTECTOR"

2 5

Animal Abuse

1990

When I offered Abu a monkey treat at the door of his cage, he took it and screamed. I grabbed Abu's furry head and held his mouth shut with my fingertips. After ten seconds, I removed my hand. Would he obey me now? No, he panicked and shrieked. I caught him and pinched his mouth closed again. Restraining most of the tension in myself, I gritted my teeth so hard that I chipped a tooth.

Abu's tiny eyes were tearing. Still, I wouldn't release him. He hadn't acquiesced to me yet. Behind his teary eyes I sensed his defiance. I suddenly felt powerful for one of the few times in my life.

Abu's darting body couldn't escape my determined grasp. I clutched the squirming monkey and kept his mouth clamped to silence his cries. I loosened my grip only when his struggle for breath weakened. He projectile vomited across the room, then began screaming again. Intent on drowning those hateful screams, I carried Abu into the bathroom and held his head under the faucet. The shock, or force of the water, silenced him, but as soon as I removed him from the water his shrieking continued. I stuck Abu's face under the water again, and again.

The frustrations I held inside since I was a boy disappeared. I no longer felt weak. I no longer felt little or sad or worthless. Or judged. I flashed upon St. Mark's church. I felt giant – like the church. I felt like the one in control, the judger, the leader, the dictator. How dare Abu not love me after I tried to love him for so long.

He would love me – or I would drown him.

How dare an animal defy me when dog and cat dander forced me to use my inhaler to breathe like other people always do so effortlessly. I loved animals – how dare they prevent me from expressing it by stopping my breath.

Abu's frightened face reminded me of my earlier trip to the thrift shop. While searching for a suitable frame for Mom's portrait, I was constantly confronted by my own nervous, needy reflection in glass and mirrors. Why did I have to be so fucking neurotic every fucking day – terrified of hurting people's feelings – paranoid about what strangers thought about my every word and reaction?

I came to Hollywood to be a movie-star, and half the time I ached to not be seen – to disappear – be invisible.

Mom, why did you disappear?

Why can't I see you?

Night after night, I ask you to come to me in my dreams, and you don't. Am I not concentrating hard enough? Catching sight of my ugly, straining face in the bathroom mirror, I demanded, "How is this for concentration?!" as I continued to force Abu under the water.

Mom, how many times did Troy hit you with that bat? Why didn't I do something to stop it?! Why didn't Dad? Why didn't Dad love me more as a kid? Was I not man enough? Why did I have a hurt a girl by pretending to date her? Why did I have to tell all the soap opera magazines I liked girls. Who made me lie? Fuck all of you. Fuck everyone who listens to every fucking straight love song on the fucking radio. Why aren't there any fucking songs about two men in love?

Fuck you for cheating on me, Rod!

When my rage was exhausted, and Abu was finally too weak to scream, I wrapped him in a towel and cradled him in my arms. He looked around desperately, trying to catch his breath. I carried him to the bed where we lay resting side by side. After he started to breathe normally, I covered him with the blankets. He fell asleep clutching my stomach.

My abusing him worked.

He loved me.

We lay together until Abu, hearing Rod return home and start watching TV in the living room, leapt up and screamed. I closed the bedroom door, so Rod wouldn't hear me jump across the bed to catch Abu. I tricked Abu into climbing under the bed, then I grabbed him and held his mouth closed until he nearly suffocated. Hyperventilating, I also struggled for air.

I needed Abu to be as weak as possible in order for our relationship to work.

In the few seconds it took the terrified animal to catch his breath, I gave him one more chance to love me. I petted his head gently. Somehow I thought he would understand that if he did things my way he wouldn't get hurt. But he shrieked so loudly that I snuck him back to the bathroom sink and repeated my heinous ritual.

I had to. I had to teach him. He had to shut up and love me, or I was going to kill him.

If Rod hadn't barged into the bathroom and rescued Abu, he might have died in my hands. The little monkey reached his exhausted, wet arms around Rod's shoulder and wheezed for life. I hated him for loving Rod, and not me.

Rod, disgusted with me, and I, disgusted with me, argued the rest of the week. Tensions escalated until, citing my friends' evidence of his affairs, I ordered him out of my house.

He left and took Abu.

Every time I entered the bathroom, I would stare at my pathetic, weak skinny face in the mirror. What had I done? Who had I become? How had this happened? I was a polite mama's boy – a straight-A student – teacher's pet - Captain of Patrol. What if I had been heterosexual and had a child? Would I have tortured my son if I felt he didn't love me? If his crying got on my nerves?

• • •

I remembered being a ten-year-old boy and having diarrhea in school.

I sat in it, afraid to admit that the foul smell was mine. My teacher politely asked me to leave the class after lunch. My mother was called to give me a ride home. My adoring, doting, angel of a mother appeared mean as she rinsed my soiled underwear in the bathroom sink. She had a disgusted look on her face. At the time, I thought she was disgusted by me, but now I understand it may have only been the odor. I told her it had been an accident. I didn't mean to humiliate myself.

That was the only time that my hero ever looked at me with disgust. My mother might have forgotten it the next day, but I never did.

How could I disappoint her like that? I was disgusting.

When I could stand this memory no longer, I rifled through more of the documents from the Kenosha Courthouse.

From Troy's Diary:

THY SHALL NOT KILL
1) pet fish - nomber unknown? Species unknown? Died because of unclean water and STARVATION...
   About 10 years of Age.
2) Pet Rabbits - ACE and THUMPER. Number of RABBITS (2) species unknown. Tourchered and killed, by starvation and cold...
   About 8-10 years of Age.
3) Turtles - number unknown? Species unknown? Painters and snappers...Killed because of Tourcher, poking with STICKS and Throwing and stepping on and Crushing.
   About 8-10 years of Age.
4) Dog (BEAGLE), KING. WATCHING FOR FRIEND when I unleashed him and he Got Away...wearabout unknown?
   About 8-10 years of Age.
5) FLYS - Number Unknown? Species unknown? Killed because of Tourcher. tearing off of wings, Sticking pins in them and burning them...
   About 8-10 years of Age. (consistently spraying pesticides)
6) ANTS - Number unknown? Species unknown? Killed because of Tourcher. Burning of Ant houses, And Spraying of poison PESTICIDES...(consistently killing Aunt Species through life, stepping on and spraying PESTICIDES)

7) GRASSHOPPERS - Number unknown? Species unknown? Killed because of suffication (pet Houses) Killed because of Tourcher, Squeezing, Tearing off of limbs... (consistently killing spicies of Grass-Hoppers Through life, walking and stepping on, Spraying of PESTICIDES...)

8) CRICKETS - Number unknown? Species unknown? Killed because of SUFFICATION (pet houses) Killed because of Tourcher, Squeezing, Tearing off of limbs... (consistently killing spicies of CRICKETS Through life, walking and stepping on, Spraying of PESTICIDES...)

9) FROGS - number unknown? Spicies unknown? Killed because of Tourcher, Killed because of SUFFICATION (pet houses) Killed because of STARVATION. (consistently Killing Species of frogs Through life...)

10) SPIDERS - number unknown? Species unknown? Tourchered and Killed, Fed To FROGS...Squashed and flushed down toilet...(consistently killing Species through life, Spraying of POISONIOS PESTICIDES AND STEPPING on them...)

11) Misquito's - Number unknown? Species unknown? Tourchered and killed... (consistently killing species Through life, swatting and spraying of POISONIOS PESTICIDES)

12) LADY BUGS - Number unknown? Species unknown? Tourchered and Killed...Kept as pets and fed to other pets...(consistently Killing of species through life, with use of poisonios PESTICIDES...)

13) CATTERPILLER'S - Number unknown? Species unknown? Tourchered and killed... Kept as pets in pet houses Sufficated and STARVED...(consistently Killing Species Through life, Spraying of PESTICIDES...)

14) BUTTERFLYS - Number unknown? Species unknown? Tourchered and Killed... Kept as pets in pet houses Sufficated and STARVED...(consistently Killing species Through life, Spraying of PESTICIDES...)

15) lightning bugs - Number unknown? Species unknown? KEPT AS PETS IN PET HOUSES, STARVED AND TOURCHERED. STEPPED ON AND Killed...(consistently killing of spicies Through use of POISON PESTICIDES...

16) WORMS - Number unknown? Species unknown? (NIGHT CRAWLERS) kept in WORM HOUSES AND CONTAINERS. refrigerated, Tourchered and Killed (STUCK HOOKS through them) USED TO LUER Fish...

17) FISH - Number unknown? Species (Bull Heads, perch, Suckers, CATFISH, BASS, Small Mouth Bass, large mouth Bass, Blue Gill, Carp...Killed for food and sport...

18) ANY OTHER SPECIES of Being I may have killed... walking STICKS SPECIES, moths species...
19) SNAKES - Number unknown? Species unknown?
20) Bees - Number unknown? Species unknown?

Ironically, with these new pages depicting Troy as a monster, I had no choice but to view him as less of a monster than I had previously. Though his abusive behavior seemed premeditated and intentional, and my abuse of Abu had surely been uncontrolled and unexpected, I'm ashamed to say I could in fact identify.

I had not "lost my mind." I knew what I was doing. Unlike what I had done to my guinea pig, this was no accident.

Why was I so pitiful a man that I relished the sense of pride in seeing my little victim fight for life in my hands? Was I so weak a man that I needed power at any expense? Did Troy feel the same primitive victory when he attacked and threatened our mother the many times before he eventually took her life? Did Troy feel powerful and god-like by beating our mother with an aluminum bat until her blood and organs filled her mouth?

I did not dare tell anyone about my actions toward Abu. They were perverse and inhuman. Unforgivable. I was a horrible human being. A waste of skin.

As uncomfortable as it was to hate myself, it was in essence an answer to a prayer. I was forced to see Troy's turmoil. Perhaps he couldn't stop hurting her? Perhaps he was so filled with weakness and frustrations that he snapped? Could he have hated himself as much as I hated myself?

It would have been so easy to go on believing that Troy and I had nothing in common: That he was the anomaly of the family. That he was inhuman or given faulty genes. But now I had way too much information to believe this previously comfortable scenario. No, Troy and I not only looked alike, but we also acted alike. We were both school misfits, both introverts with dangerous tempers, both secret abusers, both gifted creatively in drawing, both gifted in writing. Sadly, disappointingly, my brother Troy and I were not on opposite sides of the spectrum at all.

We were practically the same person.

"HEARING VOICES"

26

Schizophrenic Cousins

1990

After Rod, I was in no hurry to find another boyfriend, but when I did I wanted one I could trust wholeheartedly. I had no time for romance. I was spending every waking moment since the day I almost killed Abu, in a self-imposed penance, analyzing my thoughts and actions to prevent my losing control ever again. I decided I needed to investigate the Bierdz and DiLetti histories of abuse so I could understand what went wrong and when, and to further understand my mother's murder. My Aunt Mary and Aunt Dianne humbly insisted bipolar disorders existed in our Italian genes. More frightening, though, was my father's lineage:

Troy Bierdz, 19, (brother) killed our mother July 14, 1989.
David Bierdz, 15, (second cousin) committed to a temporary asylum.
Hal Bierdz, 33, (second cousin) diagnosed paranoid schizophrenic.

I learned that David and Hal Bierdz were both emotionally abused by their late father, Keith Bierdz.

But we weren't.

Were we?

I began to call my father and dig for family history. When he suggested coming to visit me, I thought it would be an excellent opportunity to corner him, look him square in his soft hazel eyes, and ask him if he abused us when we were younger.

Gregg picked up our father at the airport. They found me on my porch. Gregg bought expensive bottles of wine for both Dad and me.

"You're late," I laughed, "I have to ground you both. You're both grounded for a week. Like we used to be as kids."

"You kids were never grounded for a week," my father laughed.

"Yes, we were," Gregg said.

I agreed, "You grounded us and gave us spankings."

"I think I need some of this fancy wine right away," my father joked.

We walked into the kitchen. Dad commented on my paintings. He was impressed with my color-wild, expressionistic, figurative works, which were similar to art he used to have framed in his Kenosha therapy office. Since I didn't know what I was going to paint when I first attacked these canvases, I wondered if the memory of his paintings were etched into my brain – did my subconscious paint them? If so, my subconscious must have created most of my work, as I rarely sat down with a specific goal or even color, in mind. As my grade school teacher surmised, I completely trusted the process; I had "faith." Only after I picked up the brush and splashed the tip with water, did I see a flash of color go off in my head. By the time I dipped my brush in whatever color I was "told" and put it on the canvas, another flash in my brain decided the size and shape to paint. I obliged. I would not know I was painting a suitcase or a boat, until it was completed. My most relaxed sessions were definitely like meditation; an hour or two later I would sit back, amused and amazed, at what my subconscious painted – usually fauvist works influenced by Matisse or postimpressionism like Van Gogh.

Dad eyed a small portrait of a scared, little face I'd been painting that was leaning against the wall. I thought it was a subconscious representation of my face, but my father must have seen it as a monkey. Staring at it, he asked, "Where's Abu? I haven't seen him since your mother's funeral."

"Rod took him when they split up," Gregg said.

"Because I abused Abu," I said. "Abu hated me."

I turned the canvas around, embarrassed my subconscious may've been revealing too much too soon.

Gregg stated, "I wanted to hit that little thing, too, Thom. He bit me."

"I almost drowned him when I lost my temper, but it's not like I *wanted* to hurt him."

My father looked surprised, and put his hand on my shoulder. It was unlike him to be physical. I was both comfortable and uncomfortable with his gesture until I saw his real motive: he was getting me out of the way of the refrigerator.

He put ice in glasses, poured the expensive wine, and we took a walk around the block. I asked my father directly if we were abused as kids. I told him I remembered getting spankings when he got home from work.

"In Chicago, she asked me to spank you and Hope whenever I got home from college to that scary apartment. She didn't want to be the bad guy, and was very stressed," he frowned.

"Mom asked you to hit them?" Gregg asked.

"If I didn't spank Thom lightly, she would beat him until his ass was red," Dad said.

I didn't remember Chicago, and did not want to believe my mother ever beat us. "I never deserved a spanking," I said, "and in Kenosha, you gave us spankings every night. I remember you did."

Dad explained, "Your grandparents disciplined your mother a lot when she was a kid so she is the one that lost it on you kids. It's a cycle." He paused a long time, then changed the subject. "Boys, this is vacation time. Let's go to a bar on Sunset."

"Mom was strict. She had too many rules," Gregg said. "She would make me write a hundred times 'I will not do this or this.' That was so lame. But she didn't hit me."

"Well," I said, defending her, "because of Mom, I know what unconditional love is. I feel for the kids who don't get a parent like that. There was never one moment in my life when I didn't believe she loved me." I didn't mention the diarrhea incident.

My father grumbled, "Your mother only loved to get things."

"Material things? What are you talking about?"

"Whatever it was she wanted. Commitment. Attention."

This devastated me, "Man, oh, man, it's a good thing I'm the one writing her screenplay."

"About your mother?" Dad looked shocked.

"So I can honor her. It's a tribute to Mom's struggle."

Gregg said, "I'll sue you, bro, if it ever gets made. You can't ruin me like that."

"What are you so worried about? This'll set the record straight. Look at the people, like Dad, who misunderstand her."

"What, the soap has-been is using the family tragedy to revive his career?" Gregg added.

"Boys," my father intervened, "nobody wants a screenplay about–"

I jumped in to change the subject, "So if Mom told you to hit us and you didn't want to...why did you?"

"She was an impossible woman with her jealousy. She was probably really angry at me for going to college, and she probably felt excluded from my life."

Gregg said, "Okay, if Thom grew up to kill *you*, it might make sense, at least Thom was hit by you. Troy was never hit by Mom though, right?"

"She never asked me to spank him," Dad said. "She had ten years of mothering experience by then and had acquired some patience."

"Oh shit," I said, accessing and upsetting memory. I remembered hitting Troy myself. "Me. I was the one."

"What are you talking about?" Gregg asked.

I continued, "Troy was probably a year old. I must have been nine. In the basement I used to build these huge cities with Lincoln Log houses, Lego hotels and Tinker Toys. I'd weave Hot Wheels tracks between the structures as roads and highways. It was like I was God, you know? I loved to create. But Troy was downstairs, I think because Mom was doing laundry in the other room. He was by me and he kept accidentally ruining my cities. I had worked so long on those cities. I couldn't believe they were being destroyed like that. I don't know what happened, but I started swinging a Hot Wheels track and I know I hit him. I'm remembering now...damn."

Gregg's voice cracked, "So Mom took it out on Dad, who took it out on you, who took it out on Troy, who took it out on Mom."

"I didn't have to hit him," I said, sick to my stomach, "I'm an abuser."

"You were nine," my father cast his eyes down. "Kids hit each other. It's normal. What isn't normal is your neurotic guilt."

The uncomfortable memory replayed before me: picking up the Hot Wheels track Troy had stumbled over, taking the long, orange, plastic whip, and smacking him with it. At the time I was overcome with rage. How dare he wreck the city I was building.

How dare he wreck my world.

2 7

Big Dog

1990

In September, after months of beating myself up for abusing Abu, and licking my wounds over Rod, my dad convinced me I needed to date again. I agreed I needed something, or someone, to make me feel like a worthwhile human being again. I'd like to say 35-year-old Gary Erxleben's honesty and simplicity were what attracted me to him, but in reality, his muscles were what I wanted wrapped around me on nights that I hated myself. The same muscles I wanted to have sex with to distract myself from my haunted memories. He was so honest, down-to-earth, and eager to please that my friends and I nicknamed him "Big Dog." He was proud of the name. He joked about being spawned from "trailer-trash." Golf course management was his career and one major interest, which started when he was a teenager collecting golf balls for a nickel each at a country club. He was as simple as Rod was complicated.

I needed simple.

Everyone in my family loved Big Dog, and so did all my friends, even my exes. Rod liked the idea of Big Dog very much. Occasionally talking to Rod on the phone, I couldn't deny the romantic spark still existed, but I refused to ever again be in a relationship without trust. Unlike Rod, Big Dog couldn't deceive me if he tried. Unfortunately, Big Dog couldn't even spell "deceive," so I lost the best Scrabble opponent I ever had when Rod left.

I didn't have time for board games anyway. I was constantly researching and rewriting the events in my mother's life – reliving them – hearing them – feeling them – seeing her disappointed face – imagining her terrified face – day after day – week after week.

I wrote at outdoor cafes, but couldn't bear waitresses looking into my eyes, and spying the knots forming in my brain, as I struggled to respond to their simple questions and pleasantries. Most patrons at these eateries were smiling or relaxing, but I was gravely serious.

One week turned into the next, and the following month I forgot my brother-in-law's birthday, then my sister's birthday. I was never big on gifts, but I always made a point of sending an irreverent card – something very offbeat, usually in another language, just because it cracked me up. Hope didn't call to remind me of their birthdays, as our mother would have. When I realized my oversight, I remembered Rod's comment: "When the mother goes, the family falls apart." I could not deny this was happening to us Bierdzes. If my mother's consciousness was the same as it had been before her death, she must have hated this.

She probably also hated that I had lost my confidence and regressed into shy Tommy Bierdz of Kenosha again, avoiding public places as often as I could. Hating myself for being awkward and unable to maintain eye contact with friends in restaurants, I started avoiding meeting friends in public. Acquaintances could easily think the tightness in my lips meant I disliked them, when it was really only my nerves dragging my smile down. I dreaded hurting anyone's – everyone's – feelings with my unintentional, uncontrollable "rudeness."

I doubted fans' praise since I had not worked as an actor for a while. I no longer believed I was attractive, and had cosmetic surgeries to make myself feel better. Pinning my ears back made me look less like a skinny kid. I had silicone injected into my jaw, and lipo of my cheeks, to square and widen my face, and look more like Gregg. Veneers gave me the Chiclet smile other soap stars had. Lipo of my stomach meant I didn't have to do sit-ups.

I thought I looked more "manly," but my friends could hardly see a difference. Big Dog didn't understand why I did it in the first place, but supported me blindly, as he always did.

Gregg would call me every couple weeks with a "dumb blonde" joke or to name-drop which celebrities he encountered at parties or which ones he slept with. Once during a family gathering he announced to everyone, "Guess who I'm banging? Andrew Dice Clay's ex." Hope, our aunts, and I said nothing; we didn't know what reaction he expected. No one in our family had ever talked about who they were "banging."

In the yesterdays of Kenosha, Gregg had appeared to be the "perfect, straight, All-American male" with no insecurities whatsoever. Golden. But since arriving in Hollywood, Gregg had not achieved his usual effortless success. He wasn't able to outshine me, like he did in Little League. Gregg needed to impress someone, but I never understood who that someone was – if it was me, or our mother, he was going about it in all the wrong ways.

My brother stopped his one-night stands after meeting Patsy Williams in 1991. She was not a celebrity, but he found her very impressive. She was as tall and beautiful as a model, dark-eyed with Spanish heritage, and richer than anyone in our family, except Gregg, ever dreamed of being.

28

Hunger Of The Beauty Queen

1991

Years before Gregg met Patsy Williams, she was a Georgia beauty queen. Most American cities hold beauty pageants, but the wealthy families in Patsy's little Georgia hometown built their daughters' lives and dreams upon them. Fathers' supplied the unlimited funds for costumes and talent lessons, while mothers' provided perfect, pristine role models of beauty and poise. The training and experience "daddy's little girl" and "mummy's princess" received on pageant runways prepared these young ladies for lives of society balls and garden parties as the future wives and mothers in this imitation plantation aristocracy.

Patsy won several beauty crowns before pursuing a dancing career in Los Angeles. After fifteen years of auditioning, she realized a Georgia crown equaled nothing special in Hollywood. Patsy loved children and began teaching dance, while also searching for the perfect husband and father her own childhood had promised. She expected to land a successful man like her own father, someone who would also love to have a playpen full of pretty babies. My handsome and charismatic brother appeared to fit easily into her fantasy family, and she quickly fell in love with him in September of 1991.

By this time, Gregg had changed jobs again and was working as an assistant at a powerful Hollywood talent agency. On the surface, he appeared undaunted by his failure as an actor, and unscarred by the tumultuous relationship he had with his former boss, the predatory and conniving

personal manager. Gregg still seemed to possess the promise and opti-
mism suggested by the *Field Of Dreams* movie poster he'd hung above
his bed.

I first met Patsy when I bumped into Gregg at the Beverly Center
shopping mall, where he was eyeing Armani suits. As an assistant to a
very big agent, he was using his charge cards to dress to impress. Patsy
was stylish in a white blouse and black leather pants; her make-up was
subtle, tasteful, expensive. She was as pretty as the Beverly Hills cheer-
leaders shopping that day at the mall, but older. She was then 33.

Gregg had already warned me, that if I ran into him with another person, not to mention that I was gay or anything related to Mom's murder.
There were dozens of would-be agents like Gregg vying for a few promo-
tions every year, and each one chosen had to project a squeaky clean image. Besides, he said, if they knew there was schizophrenia in the family,
they'd fire him. Gregg also felt the underdog because he believed rival
assistants were likely promoted because of nepotism.

Having been warned to keep my mouth shut, I let him and Patsy do
the talking.

It was immediately evident Patsy was interested in Gregg more than
he was interested in her. During the five minutes we chatted, she was very
conscious of how she was perceived by Gregg, me, and the other men
walking by in the mall. It was a nice change for me to see someone else be
so insecure, especially someone who appeared to have everything. Later I
discovered Patsy's insecurities started when she was five, when her father
left home and divorced her mother. Heartbroken, Patsy naturally had issues with men and abandonment ever since.

Her jealousy had scared away many marriage prospects, but she was
determined to hold on to Gregg, even though she incorrectly believed he
was eight years younger than she.

After landing the job at the talent agency, Gregg began telling everyone he was 25, instead of 27. He believed the agents controlling his future
would think 27 was too old for an assistant; he thought he should've been
a full-fledged agent by 27. Since as an actor I had shaved a few years off
my age at times, I couldn't fault Gregg for his career decision. What I

didn't understand though, was his making me swear not to tell Patsy his true age. I thought it was a bit bizarre, keeping this information from the person he said he loved – someone who loved him and shared everything with him.

Being the son of a psychotherapist had its advantages. I learned to be analytical about myself, and others. I learned the meaning of "transference" when my father used to accuse my mother of "transferring" her neediness onto him. I could see that Patsy was transferring her own neediness and trust issues onto Gregg. But Patsy was also the recipient of Gregg's growing trust issues. How could he believe any woman after the primary female figure in his life, our mother, promised always to be there for him, then vanished?

During our enjoyable, analytical conversations, I told Patsy Mom had doted on Gregg. She'd always provided for him, even financially when he needed it. I feared that Gregg, perhaps subconsciously, was seeking surrogate maternal support in his relationship with Patsy. I also feared her multi-million-dollar bank account was seductive to a man who had yet to prove he could provide for himself long-term. Gregg probably thought Patsy's money was the "easy" way to achieve the successful, luxurious lifestyle he envisioned for himself.

I too dreamed of a luxurious life, but unlike Gregg, I insisted on earning it for myself. I would never give control of my life to another person for money, even though I'd almost gone through all my savings from *Y&R*. Instead of getting a real job I wanted to remain focused on my writing, and use my free time to paint, so I sold my house and lived on the profit.

Big Dog asked me to move into his condo, but I insisted on paying five-hundred-dollars a month rent, so I could maintain my independence. His place wasn't as grand as Patsy's mansion, but it was one of the nicest places I'd ever lived. The condo was modern with windows on the ceiling (great for painting) and brand new white carpeting (not so great for painting). It was comfortable, and with Big Dog's love, it seemed like his home was my home.

29

Serial Killer Happy Hour

<u>**1991**</u>

In October, I called to check in with my friend Gary Scheuerman. My Wisconsin cowboy always supported and encouraged my career goals and new romances. Over the years the bonds formed during our relationship deepened into something more spiritual. Gary approved of Big Dog and thought his energy perfectly balanced mine.

Gary was bored after almost twenty years of bartending: listening to the same disco hits played way too loud, and pouring the same mixed drinks to the same customers, some of whom had become friends, but most of them just became alcoholics. It was depressing for him to spend so much time in a pick-up environment, especially when he watched many of his good-natured patrons slowly die of AIDS. We were both grateful to be HIV negative. The heavy subject of AIDS turned our conversation spiritual. We talked about his Native-American ancestry, sweat lodges, and healing energies.

Gary also shared one of his psychic episodes with me.

A year earlier, he was wiping the counter of the quiet basement bar at Club 219, when he suddenly heard a "voice" tell him there was a serial killer in his presence. Gary turned quickly, but the only other person in the bar was a regular customer he had served many times before. Gary knew the "voice" wasn't the customer's, and he didn't believe this quiet, bearded, blond guy was a killer.

Gary tried to put the incident out of his mind. No one was more spooked or surprised than he when this same regular customer, Jeffrey

143

Dahmer, was arrested for multiple murders a few months later. Gary felt terrible he hadn't gone to the police.

I assured Gary they would not have believed him.

I never had reason to doubt Gary's honesty, and I'd always respected the *possibility* of his psychic abilities. However, from this point forward I would never again begin to even question his "messages."

30

The Message

1994

G ary and I talked at least once a year to share what was new in our lives. I'd called him in 1993 when I got acting job – playing a murderer on an episode of *Matlock*. We also discussed how I was settling into a "routine" life with Big Dog at his condo in Valley Village, half-an-hour north of Hollywood.

Gary phoned to tell me when he quit bartending and bought a quiet ranch above Green Bay in Door County wilderness. He lived there with a hot Wisconsin cowboy of his own named Scott. During the summer they ran a restaurant in the high-tourist area. The only time they really had to see people was during the four warm months of the year when their restaurant was open. Other than that, they had their horses and dogs to keep them busy, and lots of wood to chop.

The last time Gary called, he was concerned because he had a vision of his German Shepherd getting hit by a truck. When he phoned in January of 1994, I was afraid he'd tell me this premonition had come true. But it was another premonition he was calling about – a more frightening premonition – and it was for me.

Gary was weeping over the phone, which was very out of character for someone so masculine. He was embarrassed, but couldn't stop himself.

"I've got to talk to you, TJ," he wailed, "I've got a message for you."

"A message?"

"I'm not sure who it's from...I think it's your mother's soul, but it could be a part of your brother's soul – or some weird combination. I'm in pain, real pain."

"I can hear that in your voice. Pain where?"

"I've never felt anything like it," Gary continued laboriously. "It's excruciating...I'm on the floor, curled over. I can't stand it."

He wept for almost a full minute. "It's horrible! You can't imagine – it's not human–"

"Shit, Gary, I'm sorry..."

"I'm supposed to feel...this...pain...to...show you...to convince...you of...their pain."

"Whose pain?"

"Theirs, I think. I don't know, hers or his or a combination, like I said, but it's all wrong. It's so fucked up," he groaned louder.

I listened to Gary groan. Finally he returned.

"Teej, I'm supposed to tell you that your mother loves you very much. 'Her four'...she keeps saying 'she loves her four.'"

"I know she loves us kids," I breathed into the phone, emotional. I felt my mother near. Goosebumps layered my arms.

"You have to save him!" Gary demanded.

"Who?"

"Oh, Teej, man, Troy's soul is...damn it!...dying."

"Troy's soul? In prison?"

"Yes. Yes. Troy is in trouble. She wants you to go to him."

"No way."

"You're the only one who can save him," he said. "She keeps saying that. His soul. It's urgent. These five years have devastated him, I guess. You have to go to him now."

I didn't say anything for quite a while as Gary repeated his words over and over. Gary did not know I'd been pleading to my mother in prayer, begging her to speak to me. Reflecting on my selfish relationship with her, I wanted to make it up to her and had been asking her if there was anything I could do for her. I had been calling on her spirit for almost five years.

"I need some time to think about this," I told Gary, coldly.

"She keeps saying you have to go. Now. If you could feel this pain."

"Why *me*?"

"She says you're the only one. Do it for her, she's begging you." After a long beat, Gary calmed himself. "The message is complete," he sighed, grateful.

"Gary, Troy severed any connection to me, to our whole family, when he killed her. As far as I'm concerned, he is dead and that's great."

"His soul is dying."

"Souls don't die," I argued.

"I never thought about that, about souls dying. I honestly hadn't," Gary said. "But she said it, they said it kind of together."

"When something dies it transforms itself, even science proves that. So an energy – Troy's – whatever it is – cannot stop. Right?"

"That's not what the message says," Gary reiterated, "don't under-estimate what just happened. I didn't ask for this. It was huge, man. The biggest thing that's ever happened to me in my life. This was a message from some very strange place."

"I believe you," I explained, "I know you."

No one in the family had maintained contact with Troy in the past four and a half years, and they expected to keep it that way. But after hear-ing Gary for half-an-hour on the phone, I could see there was no way to refuse him and avoid seeing Troy. The more adamantly he insisted I see Troy, the more terrified I became of that possibility. Troy had been as dead to our family emotionally, as we had prayed he were physically. If Troy was not dead, and Gary's message seemed to say he was not, wouldn't Troy be a hardened bully in a prison gang, probably killing inside those walls? He had lifted weights, and his years in Tae Kwon Do class prob-ably assured him a place in the prison hierarchy, so why the fuck was I supposed to visit him? I mean, what was Troy really like now – in 1994? Why did Mom want me to go to him? It didn't make any sense.

That night, in between nightmares of being murdered, I lay awake tossing. In the past five years, and for the next decade to come, to the chagrin of every boyfriend I had, I couldn't sleep at night for more than two hours in a row.

The next morning while Big Dog nervously paced, I phoned the Columbia Correctional Prison and talked to Admittance to check out the situation. The person on the phone said he had to send an officer to Troy, who was housed in the psychiatric unit, to get his permission to see me. On TV shows, I had seen visitors face prisoners with thick glass between them. That thought comforted me slightly, but still I wondered what does Troy have to lose by using his black belt skills to break through the glass and attack me? He was already sentenced to life in prison. He had made it clear that he hated me, and could now deliver on his threat to rip out my heart in six seconds and hold it in front of my face until I died.

Was it because he and I looked more alike than any others in the family? Was he still jealous of my past success? Was he even more threatened by my homosexuality? Did his hate grow, because, like our mother, I intervened – and even had him live under my roof, and insisted he follow my rules – in expectation of him maturing?

If Troy finally decided to act on his threats, I would be dead unless the guards took less than six seconds to draw their guns and fire.

Big Dog pleaded with me not to go. As much as I loved him, I was very independent and not about to listen to him. Our relationship was a case of opposites attracting, and I didn't include him in on much of my life because he simply wouldn't understand it.

Neither would Gregg. When I told him about the message, he didn't believe it. He said I deserved to die if I did something as stupid as seeing Troy.

I received the prison's clearance to visit. I also received Troy's indirect permission through Mike Grove, one of the prison's psychiatric counselors. For my safety, I requested Mike be present when I saw Troy.

Ignoring Big Dog's anxious concern, I reserved a flight for January 16. My return flight would be twenty-four hours later. I decided that was plenty of time to land in Milwaukee, rent a car, drive to the middle of Wisconsin, and see Troy.

"THE BRIDGE"
(In the collection of Wil Perdue)

31

Facing Troy

January 16, 1994

The temperature was unimaginably cold when I landed at Mitchell Field Airport. I got a Taurus rent-a-car and zigzagged small, icy highways northwest for three hours. I passed many deserted barns, and got lost for fifteen minutes in the state's biggest tourist site, the Wisconsin Dells. January was out-of-season, and the below-zero temperatures kept everybody indoors, except for a few gambling-addicts heading for the nearby Ho-Chunk Indian Casino.

My destination was between the Fox and the Wisconsin Rivers. One flowed north, the other south. The two were separated by a narrow piece of land over which Indians, trappers, and traders traveling the waterways had to portage, or carry, their canoes and heavy packs from one stream to the next. The settlement that grew there would become known as Portage. Portage had less than ten thousand residents, including the thousands of people either working for or incarcerated at the maximum security Columbia Correctional Prison. This city named for "carrying baggage" seemed a fitting place to house the most dangerous criminals in Wisconsin; men obviously carrying heavy emotional baggage. Jeffrey Dahmer was one of them.

I parked in the lot of the colossal penal colony, noticing the guards on lookout posts with machine guns. As I walked past the electrical fences, a buzzer sounded and the prison doors opened electronically.

In the brick foyer, a ceiling camera inspected me as I stomped the snow off my shoes. After what seemed like an eternity, another electric buzzer sounded and allowed me through a second set of security doors into Admittance.

A burly guard stood behind a bulletproof window. He passed me a form through the small opening and said, "Write the inmate's name here."

I looked at the form. My hand trembled over the space marked "relationship to inmate." I wrote "brother" but I felt like I was about to see a stranger.

The guard approved my ID. "Here's a key to a locker."

I crossed the room and read the rules stating I was only allowed to carry five dollars in change into the visiting area. I put my jacket, car keys, and wallet into the locker, then walked through the metal detector.

The guard stamped my hand and led me through a black-lit security room with double electric doors. I asked if Mike, the psychiatric unit counselor, had arrived yet for my visit. The guard said he didn't know.

The guard returned to Admittance, the double electric doors closing behind him. Across from me, the doors to the visiting room slowly opened. Cautiously, I stepped into the enormous room and looked around. No one was there. Mike had not arrived yet. Would he arrive at all?

As I waited, I studied the visiting area more closely. The room contained forty small, open clusters of tables and chairs. Nothing separated the chairs from each other – no partitions – no glass – no protection.

I turned around thinking, "Hey! No! You can't let him in the same room with me! He'll kill me!"

I heard a woman's voice say, "Come this way."

It was a female guard with a notepad and wearing a headset.

"Hi," I said, "my brother...who's in here...and I always had this... trouble between us."

Preoccupied with her headset, she led me through the large room. My heart beat faster the farther away she took me from her large, circular guard desk. I looked over my shoulder and saw that behind her desk was a glass wall through which was what looked to be the search room and

entrance for the prisoners. Overhead was a large clock. The sharp movement of the minute hand caught me by surprise.

We were walking the gymnasium-sized room, passing a microwave
squeezed between vending machines humming with enough electricity to
keep food refrigerated. This irritating high-pitched buzzing amplified the
cold institutional sterility. Farther along the wall, a glass case displayed
watercolor landscapes and knitted Green Bay Packer-themed clothing
made by inmates. A playpen with children's toys was set against another
wall, and behind that area were windows overlooking the bleak, snowy
exercise yard.

The guard said, "I have a note to call Mike Grove in for your visit.
You're assigned to Table 36."

My mouth went dry. I sat on the blue upholstered wooden chair. Its
arm touched the arm of the next chair – the chair where Troy would sit.

Maybe I would die of fright before Troy got a chance to kill me.

The guard walked back across the room to her desk. I flinched as an
inmate appeared at the search window. I saw a crazy man's face covered
by a scraggly beard and wild, long, dark hair. Was it Troy? A smile crept
across this haunted face. I panicked as my head flushed with heat and my
eyes teared.

I prayed silently to God. I asked to be saved and protected. I wondered if I was meant to be dead in a minute. I'd asked for it after all. In
the five years since Mom's death, I had read every book I could find on
life-after-death, and dissatisfied with the vague and predictable scenarios,
I'd demanded Mom come to me and show me what life-after-death was.
When she didn't, I demanded God do it. "Fuck," I thought, "I went too
far." I apologized, and begged God to keep me alive. I wasn't ready to
die.

Petrified, I sat trapped in the prison visiting room, with nothing to
separate or protect me from Troy once he was allowed to enter.

The guard at the desk waited for a signal, then buzzed in Troy. He
crept into the room, wearing a worn green cotton uniform. His hair was
matted to his head. Part of his face was visible through a two-inch section

where his beard was shaved, or the whiskers had been pulled out. I could smell his stench from across the room. As he came nearer, I saw his eyes were dark and hollow. His smile exposed brown and yellow teeth.

Troy said, "J.I.A. folder a hutch. To be cardboard – if eyes laughing. I'm taller than you."

I didn't know how to react to that.

An attractive, longhaired man with a longer beard, slight belly, and bifocals entered and introduced himself as Mike, the prison counselor. Though I was comforted by his presence, I quickly realized he was not likely to offer me any additional physical protection. Instead of Troy killing just me in six seconds, he would now kill both of us in twelve.

Troy didn't know where to sit. He babbled on, looking terrified.

"Face is on the right side. Faces are on the right side – keep the sounds on the right to look at." He spoke gibberish to the floor, rolled an invisible cigarette, put it to his mouth, then realized it didn't exist.

"You're not going to kill me, are you?" I asked.

The guard at the desk wasn't even looking at us.

Mike sat with pen and paper, passively watching Troy and me. He adjusted his glasses and said, "Troy, your brother flew here from California."

Troy's yellow teeth grinned, but he didn't seem to hear. He fidgeted in his green cotton shirt and scanned the room in a paranoid manner. His matted hair smelled stale, and stuck to the shaved section of his face. His eyes stared at me, but there was nothing in them.

Troy spoke gibberish and looked around. The only word I could make out was "TV."

Mike explained, "I think he thinks he's on TV."

Troy didn't know where to sit. Mike indicated a chair. Troy sat, looking terrified, and babbled on.

"What is it like in here?" I asked.

He looked at me, shaken. I breathed, relieved, realizing that my brother was too pitiful to be dangerous.

"Do you know who this is?" Mike asked.

"Tommy," he said.

"You've never been in this room before?" I asked. "No visitors in four and a half years?"

Mike checked his paper, "This is his first time here."

Troy looked lost.

"It's the visiting area," I explained. "Mom asked me to come."

He nervously looked at the visitor entrance. In his distorted state perhaps he expected our mother to be there.

Mike said, "I'll be Troy's counselor."

"Who," I asked, "has been counseling him before?"

"There is only one counselor assigned per unit. About sixty inmates. But there really was no reason to counsel Troy before this since he kept to himself."

"So nobody's even talked to him for five years?"

Mike explained, "The report says he didn't need any contact. He usually just lies on the floor and stares at the ceiling."

Troy mumbled, "At – the ceiling changes when I look there - changes into screaming bugs."

Mike said, "He earns several dollars a month for not causing trouble like the other ones do, don't you, Troy? Which goes to tobacco – you can tell from his teeth and fingers. His warden told me Troy did not choose to leave his cell unless he was forced to."

"Is he worried about gangs or something?" I asked.

Mike explained, "The gangs stay away from the inmates in the psychiatric unit."

"Troy," I said, "can I get you something to drink?"

Mike pointed to the vending machines, "Soda pop, coffee."

"Troy, can I get you something?"

I was stunned and saddened to see that Troy seemed to have no idea what my question meant. Or maybe he understood me, but didn't know if he was allowed something from a vending machine. I had no idea Troy had been so neglected. My eyes welled up as I edged over to the vending machines.

I bought a hot chocolate, brought it to Troy, then nervously spilled some and scalded his arm. Troy didn't react at all. He didn't even seem to feel the blistering liquid. How was that possible?

"Hot chocolate," I explained, "...for you."

Troy looked amazed and glanced to Mike for approval.

I asked Mike what medication Troy was on. He told me that Troy was not on anything. Later I discovered they had not even officially diagnosed him. They were confused from the court records how to classify Troy. They might never have treated him, I imagined, as long as he had lain in his cage and hadn't done anything disruptive. I was also told that a family member had to request that an inmate receive medication.

It was becoming evident why Gary's message was phrased the way it was: "Your mother says you're the only one who can save him." Not only was I the only one who would pay attention to paranormal contact, and feel that I owed her enough to follow up on it, but I was also the only one in the family who could identify with such an outsider.

I asked for Troy to be put on medication. Mike agreed to speak to the doctor, then went to the guard desk.

Troy had no idea what to do with his empty cup. He spoke more gibberish, then looked around for cameras, still believing he was being filmed.

It wasn't my concern for his well-being motivating my efforts to bring him back to a lucid state. I had questions for him to answer.

After babysitting the shell of Troy for two more hours, I met Mike at the desk. He said the doctor would prescribe Troy Chlorpromazine to cut back psychotic symptoms such as disassociation and hallucinations, but his paranoia would probably remain.

"How fast does this pill work?" I asked.

"In some cases there could be a noticeable change in twenty-four hours."

After Mike left, I sat with Troy. I wanted to ask him about the murder, but he wasn't in his right mind. I walked over to investigate the bookshelf by the guard desk. Finding only Bibles and Sears catalogues, I meandered to the children's area where I discovered a bigger selection of books and toys. I was stunned to find Lincoln Logs, and decided to take them back to our table. I built a house with them, much like the houses I used to build when I was 9-years-old. Much like the houses Troy accidentally knocked over.

I was filled with guilt and emotion, but Troy's look bounced from skittishness to boredom. I asked him if he remembered the cities I made when I was a kid. He didn't. I asked him if he remembered me striking him with a Hot Wheels track.

He didn't.

My breath became asthmatic.

I asked him if he had a TV or radio in his cell. He didn't. I asked him if I could buy them for him. He didn't know. I told him I would check with Mike.

I asked him if he had any questions about our family members. He didn't.

When our time was up, I hugged him goodbye.

He wanted to know if I was going to see him again.

I said yes.

"RED HEALING"
(In the collection of David Wareham)

32

Sibling Pieces

January 16, 1994

L eaving Troy's prison, I was grateful to be alive and amazed that he didn't try to kill me. Driving faster than I should've been, I sped through the snow and past the evergreens dancing in the wind, reminding me I was in a winter wonderland. This helped me catch my breath. I wanted to stop the car and make a snowball, but I was anxious to get to my sister's house and surprise her with the news of our mother's message and my seeing Troy. I'd only told Hope I was in Wisconsin for one day, and asked to spend the night at her place.

I wondered how Gregg in Los Angeles would react to me seeing Troy and surviving.

I kept thinking about Troy's psychotic eyes and his scattered words. He couldn't possibly be faking that, could he? Mike had verified Troy's "deadness" in his cell these past years. He couldn't possibly be faking a psychotic mind all this time, merely hoping I would show up so he could kill me in a subsequent visit, could he? He certainly hadn't tried to kill me when the guards were way across the room and he had the chance.

Dreading the sadness in my sister's eyes when I brought up the subject of Troy, I was filled with frustration and nerves. I wanted to turn around, drive north to the Indian casino, and play the slot machines. Gambling and sex took my mind off my problems, because they forced me to concentrate on something else – something pleasurable. But Big Dog wasn't around for sex, and I took a pass on the slot machines because my sister expected me for supper. I resigned myself to the fact that, once again, I would be a nervous wreck all night.

By the time the highway was completely blanketed in snow, my rent-a-car's lights broke through the blackness, and shined on my sister's brick home. The car skidded into the frozen hedges. Hope, shivering and holding her 1-year-old daughter, Julia, and Sam greeted me at the door. I asked how their business, a frozen yogurt store, was doing. Without listening to the response, I whispered, "Mom made me come see Troy."

Hope's smile fell. She was clearly crushed.

"I saw Troy," I whispered, shaking the snow off my shoes and entering her living room.

She looked at me like she had no idea who I was.

"Tommy, you don't make any sense."

"You don't always make sense, you know. Who opens a frozen yogurt store in Wisconsin?" I hugged her.

"Everybody makes mistakes."

"That's what I'm talking about," I said, "like Troy made mistakes."

I commented on the new birdhouses in her collection, as they led me to their kitchen, passing blank walls "calling out" for art. I had offered them paintings, but they didn't think my bold colors fit their décor. Once in the kitchen, Hope and Sam fastened Julia into her highchair.

Hope whispered, "I don't want to hear about Troy."

"He can't escape this time. There's electrical fences. Come with me tomorrow and see the guards and all the barbed wire."

Sam opened a beer and whispered to me, "You're not going back to see him again, are you?" But he could tell by my expression I was.

"Beer?" he asked.

"Tequila," I answered.

Hope poured me a drink, then put the pepper steak on the table. "I don't understand you, Tommy. First the gay thing, then silicone in your jaw, and now this."

"Hope, he's going to tell me what happened that night."

"We know what happened that night," she said, shaking her head in disgust.

During supper, Hope occasionally disappeared into the bathroom, then returned with red, swollen eyes. She exchanged secret glances with

Sam, giving me reason to feel paranoid. She made up the couch for me to sleep on, and hugged me before she went to bed.

As usual, I lay awake much of that night. I knew my sister was also lying awake, terrified. I wondered how I could help her get sleep? How could I reassure her, and get her to realize Troy was never going to hurt her again – she had nothing to fear from him?

I knew she had nightmares about Troy. We all did. Nightmares he would kill us. And she must have had nightmares that he would kill Julia. If she weren't going to see for herself that Troy was in a prison where it was impossible to escape, I would have to show her secondhand. I would have to get her photos.

The next morning, Big Dog, sounding extremely frightened, woke us all up very early with a phone call. He thought he could have died in the 6.7 magnitude earthquake that struck Los Angeles. I told Big Dog that although I wasn't in Los Angeles, I'd experienced an earthquake of my own – in Portage. His quake was centered near his condo in Northridge. His skylights shook like crazy, scaring him out of bed, and some wall mirrors and plaster cracked. He desperately wanted me with him, but I told him I absolutely had to stay in Wisconsin.

After Hope went to work, Sam cleaned the breakfast dishes and I rescheduled my return flight. I then drove up to Portage, bought a camera, and from my car outside the prison grounds, I took pictures of the two-story barbed wire fences and the sign reading "Electrical Fence." I took photos of the guards and their machine guns. I parked and joined the few visitors standing in line, waiting to enter.

In the visiting area Troy and I were assigned to Table 14, near the vending machines. Right behind us was the window covered with icicles. Troy was one of four prisoners being visited, the three others were scattered at faraway tables. Although the medication seemed to have improved his competency significantly, he was the only prisoner not competent enough to have worn a T-shirt under his green uniform. He shivered. I stared at the goose bumps on his arms and the many cigarette burn marks under self-carved tattoos on his biceps. I could only imagine how alone and tortured he was, and had been, through various stages of his life. I wanted him to trust me, and not see me as an outsider.

"Remember *The Twilight Zone*?" I asked.

"People and aliens," he said.

"In some of them," I said. "You know, maybe it's because I used to watch *The Twilight Zone*, and maybe they had an episode that spooked me, as some of them can do, but I believed way back then that I was the only living human being. That everybody else, except Mom, were robots waiting for me to let my guard down, and that they'd 'get me' when I did. Like it was a huge conspiracy to get me."

"They could've gotten your eyes out when you were sleeping."

I patted his back, "I never thought about that."

"People get killed. Robots."

"I don't think that's really true. Do you really think there are robots killing people?"

His silence and anxious glances around the room told me he did think that. I was tempted to agree with him, so that he would see me as an ally, but I thought sustaining this lie might do him more harm than good.

I changed the subject, asking, "Think it's time for popcorn?"

He seemed alarmed, "No. Just sit. We can't move around all the time."

"You sit. I'll go get me a decaf cappuccino." I eyed the vending machine, then added, "I guess a plain coffee."

Troy held me in place. "Sit here."

"Oh...okay."

We sat in silence, aside from the shrill electrical buzzing. I heard his breathing, and I knew he was listening to mine because he altered his to coincide. He searched for an invisible cigarette, got angry with himself, sat back, studied me, and tried discreetly to imitate the way I crossed my legs. Then, very slowly, as if he didn't want me to notice, he parted his hair like mine. I was flattered. Troy had never liked anything about me in the past. This was a welcome change.

As if he were reading my mind, he said, "We never got along."

"You weren't very easy...to like," I told him.

"Why did I come to see you? In jail?" he asked.

I was stunned. He didn't know he was the one in jail? How was I going to tell him that he was? He looked so fragile.

"Let's think about that," I said. "Let's look at our clothes, then the clothes of the other people."

"One person at every table that's wearing...my green outfit, I'm the one? In jail?"

Not knowing what to say, I just looked at him.

He said, "I had a security guard job. You got jail because you're gay."

"Not quite. Can you think back to July 14, 1989?"

He had no idea what I was talking about.

"Mom's last night," I reminded him.

"Her last night?"

"On that night. The kitchen. I saw the 'after' photos, but only you guys were there. So fill me in."

He stared at the ceiling, not blinking for an entire minute.

"You don't remember?" I asked. "What happened? Between you and Mom?"

He had no idea.

"You don't know why you're in jail?"

He didn't.

"Troy...after I kicked you out, she took you home to Wisconsin. Don't you remember that? That was in 1988. Then in 1989 you...hurt Mom. You hurt her."

He interrupted me, "I hurt her? That's a dream I keep having."

"I'm not gonna put up with a liar. You honestly don't remember? Calling 911 and saying *I* hurt Mom and that *I* raped you too? Why would you try to frame *me*?"

"I need a smoke."

"Smoking's bad for you."

"Can I get ice cream?"

"No. You're already too cold. You should have worn a T-shirt. Why didn't you?"

He looked confused. I pointed to my T-shirt.

He said, "My name is like Ted Bundy. No lie. I like it up there in writing, kind of like you and the magazine covers."

I stood up, saying, "Make sure you see Mike all you can. And take your pills. I'm sorry, but I don't want to help you anymore unless you can remember what happened July 14th."

He avoided my eyes.

I walked toward the guard desk, turning around to see if he would look at me. He wouldn't. Time to get back to L.A. anyway.

Outside the prison, I called Big Dog from a freezing phone booth. I told him I hated that Troy was playing games with me. I hated that it was all so unresolved.

I dropped the film off at a drugstore and bought a card that I'd send to Hope with the photos the next day. Driving through wintry, old-fashioned Portage, I imagined many old-fashioned girls, like Hope, in these little old-fashioned houses. They were probably baking old-fashioned chocolate-chip cookies or getting ready for dates. None of their brothers killed their mothers.

I pulled my hair as hard as I could. I didn't know why. But I kept doing it as I drove. It felt good because it felt bad. When no other cars were in listening distance, I screamed. I screamed full voice for fifteen minutes, pulling my hair. I found myself at a park.

The nine-acre park was the most picturesque in Portage. The empty preserve had a frozen fishing pond and a bridal arch. A plaque stated the bridal arch was erected when a young couple on their honeymoon missed the turn and drowned in the pond.

How fucking unfair, I thought.

33

Scalding

I had to see Troy again – just one more time. I needed him to give me information, to say something about the night he killed Mom. We were stationed far away from the guard desk, by the microwave. Troy remembered to wear his T-shirt. He looked nervously at the other visitors, then said, "Want to know how I made you come back?"

"You made me come back?"

"Want to know how?"

"Sure."

"I am thinking, but not sure really, if I control you."

"I see. Well. Hmmm. You smell better. Did you take a nice hot bath?"

"There are no bathtubs in here, Tommy."

"Well. Jail is supposed to be a punishment, you know."

He looked down to the floor.

"Hey," I smiled, "I got you a surprise cooking."

I rose to go to the microwave where I'd put in a vending machine pizza, but he looked so panic-stricken that I sat again. I whispered, "I already checked them out. They're not robots."

Troy wasn't so sure. Several visitors continued to look at us, but perhaps they were waiting for the microwave, which beeped. I rose to go to it.

Returning to Troy, I handed him the sizzling pizza wrapped in napkins. He took off the napkins and held the pizza, scalding his bare hands.

He opened four salt packets and poured them all on his small pizza. Did he always use that much salt? Judging from his sour face as he chewed, he was definitely not used to that much salt.

"Troy. You can brush some salt off. Okay?"

He looked amazed at the possibility. I wiped the salt off.

"Try it now."

He nodded, eating slowly, as the pizza burned his mouth.

"From now on," I suggested, "just half a packet of salt, okay?"

"Half a packet."

I sat next to Troy and put my arm around him. Wanting to make sure he didn't misconstrue my touching him, I said, "This isn't a gay thing – me touching you."

"I'm not gay," he said, "Mom said she couldn't take two gay sons."

I was surprised to hear that, and didn't know what it meant. "It wouldn't matter if you were," I said, tapping his shoulder unconsciously as my arm relaxed around him. But my eyes kept returning to the rule sheet that said "No physical contact." I removed my arm.

Troy and I sat talking about pizza for about an hour. I enjoyed being with him. I couldn't explain why. He was just comfortable to be near. Later we drew with crayons. He drew a red karate expert. I drew a happy yellow house, outlined it in red, then orange, then green, then blue. After we finished drawing, I led Troy past the glass cabinets and pointed to the knit slippers with Packers insignias.

"You could do that," I said.

"Do what?"

"Knit. If you learned how."

"Like Grandma DiLetti?"

"Yeah."

"Only girls knit."

I laughed, and couldn't stop smiling at his innocence. "Men prisoners have done these. See their names?"

Troy read the names and was shocked. "Like Rosie Greer?"

"Sure. I bet they have a class to teach knitting here, huh?" I said.

Irritated, he looked for and apparently found his invisible cigarette. "Sometimes men knit slippers?" he asked in disbelief, as if I were deliberately lying to him.

"Sure." I bought him a candy bar and watched him relax and drool as he savored it slowly. He wrapped and unwrapped the uneaten portion many times. Then he focused on me.

Everything seemed easy – almost as if it were in slow motion.

"Tommy," he said, "I thought we were done being brothers."

"I know. I thought that too." To avoid crying, I stared at the guard and pretended to be him for a few minutes, sitting in a no-nonsense uniform. When I was composed and back to being me, I browsed the children's books. I pulled out *The Little Mermaid*.

Back at our table, I read out loud from the book, showing Troy the pictures.

Later I asked the guard to snap a Polaroid of us. Inmates are allowed two photos per visit, and money is withdrawn from their accounts to pay for them. Troy had never shown interest before, but he did then, and since I just put a few dollars in his account, he complied. I'd never been so relaxed getting my picture taken, and I had done plenty of photo shoots.

Troy asked later, "Can you get a cell next to mine?"

"I don't think so. But that would be cool. Like when we had friends over when we were little."

"We could play checkers, like Grampa."

"I don't think they'll let us."

"It doesn't seem fair."

"I know."

"Nothing's fair." He stared at the garbage can.

I stared at it too, then agreed, "Nope. Nothing's fair."

• • •

That night at the Portage Motor Inn, a long rectangle of a building overlooking the highway, I ignored the blinking phone message light. I was overwhelmed with new emotions, and didn't want to deal with any messages. I didn't want to hear if Big Dog had discovered more earth-quake damage, or if Gregg had called to tell me he disapproved of my visiting Troy, or if Hope couldn't sleep because of my coming back to Wisconsin and stirring up the past.

I walked to the window and opened the drapes. Outside, unlike Los Angeles where there are thousands of buildings, there was only a single highway in the distance. Lonely lights moved to and fro between patches of evergreens. I studied the sporadic smears of traffic lights. The phone rang. Ignoring it, I walked into the bathroom.

I sat on the edge of the cold porcelain bathtub, examining it. How many baths had I taken in my life? They were a meditative attempt of mine to break up the day. What would I do without a bathtub? I couldn't imagine being denied that. What else did I take for granted that Troy had to live without now, and for the rest of his life? My brother, only 23, would never again know the comfort of being submerged entirely in heated water, unless as a very old man when he was freed.

I turned on the hot water and stuck my hand under the scalding stream. Troy somehow didn't mind scalding liquid. How was that possible? The water was killing me. My hand was bright red, but I kept it there, imagining what it was like to be him. What was it like to have shut off your feelings of physical pain? I began to admire Troy for the first time; he certainly had determination to have built up a pain threshold to the extent that he had. Could Troy also shut off all his other feelings?

That night, I gambled at Ho-Chunk slot machines, but it was Troy, not triple-7's, I saw in front of me. Occasionally, *Y&R* fans recognized me and came over to introduce themselves, or say they missed my character Phillip, dead now for five years. Drinking heavily, I tried to be cordial and appreciative to these fans, and wiping the tears from my face, I didn't explain my emotions were a family matter. Driving back to the hotel, I realized they probably saw me as a drunken soap opera has-been, crying because I was penniless.

But that's not who I was at all.

At least not yet.

I was anxious to surprise Troy with another visit. And it amused me to wonder if he would still think he had controlled me to come.

The following day, I warmed my hands around my coffee, as I sat next to Troy at Table 27 by the vending machines.

"What happened that night?" I asked.

"I don't know," he said, "I blacked out."

"You blacked out? You really did? No lies, remember?"

He made a motion with his hands above his head. I had no idea what it meant. I whispered, "You think about it while I get us a book or some crayons."

Angry, I ambled toward the bookshelf by the guard desk. A pretty woman in a gray suit entered the room, and introduced herself as Dr. Green. She explained she would prescribe and monitor Troy's medication while the counselor, Mike, would provide most of his therapy. Dr. Green asked if Troy had any reaction to the pills he'd started taking.

I watched her talk to Troy. He avoided her eyes. She told me that he wasn't having side effects.

"I hear you are from California," she said, friendly.

"Yeah," I smiled.

"Mike can see to it that Troy has three twenty-minute calls a week to you in Los Angeles, if that's something you would like."

I looked at Troy, who was avoiding my eyes. "I don't know. I mean I'm not sure it would do any good."

Getting her alone by the guard desk, I explained I was upset Troy was holding back information from me. I asked her if the medicine he was taking might prompt him to reach out more to me. I asked what the chances were that he would call me in Los Angeles and apologize for killing our mother.

Dr. Green looked deflated, "You expect him to be sorry?"

"He has to be."

"Boys who commit matricide rarely are. And they don't usually reach out or call. Brings up too much emotion for them." She gave me a sympathetic smile and left.

I found myself in the children's area with *The Little Mermaid* again. When I sat next to Troy, I put my arm around him.

The guard walked over to us and said that visitors were not allowed to touch inmates, except for embraces at the beginning and end of their visits. I withdrew my arm.

After a while, I said, "Dr. Green is sexy, huh?"

"The sexy ones are spies. How long do I have to see her?"

"I think an hour."

"You're not listening. How long am I in here?"

"In here? Nobody talked to you about this?"

"I can get the security job back at CBS. Mom has my uniform back at home."

"Mom's dead, Troy. You killed her."

"I killed her?"

"Stop it. Please. And her house is sold."

"But it's my house. Mom promised."

"You don't get a house if you kill somebody."

"I was thinking when I get out of here I could have the master bedroom and rent out the other ones."

"Forever...you'll be locked up. Forever or close to that. You screwed up things real good that night with Mom."

He looked crushed. He appeared to be hearing his life sentence for the first time. I started to lecture him, "Don't you feel bad about what you did?"

"She asked for it," he said.

As if our mother had asked to be beaten to death with a bat.

"Is that why you're the first person in Wisconsin to be denied parole for fifty years? All the other guys you see in here – I bet every one of those guys will get out before you."

I quickly walked to the guard desk and declared that I was ready to leave. I gave Troy an obligatorily hug, saying, "I'm leaving for L.A. in a few hours. You create your life, Troy. I created a life out there. You created one in here."

I walked out, not looking back.

80 Eyes

1994

My reunion with Troy, however tense and unresolved, brought a new openness to my spirit. Feeling bigger, more connected, and confident I began auditioning again, and won guest-starring roles on *Melrose Place* and *Murder, She Wrote*. I portrayed an abusive boyfriend in one and a sympathetic killer in the other. After seeing Troy in life, I was strangely "playing" him on TV.

My new confidence did not mean I was comfortable on the set – far from it. I was noticeably more nervous than the other actors, and even though I was once again achieving my lifelong dream, I was not enjoying it. My performances received a good response, but to me they felt forced and artificial. Acting wasn't filling the holes that were still inside me.

For as long as I can remember, I have been an ill-at-ease misfit for at least fifteen minutes every hour, desperately wanting to change into my carefree brother Gregg during that dark, discomforting quarter-hour, yearning to have the ease and simplicity of Big Dog's wide smile around the clock. I could never justify paying for therapy because of Mom's remarks about therapists, meaning Dad, being suspect. Plus being a paranoid child, I had grave trust issues and couldn't fathom *surrendering* to any authority. At that time, I would never take medication because of all the mental work I had done to achieve forty-five centered minutes each hour. I feared taking the wrong pill would undo all my years of hard mental balancing, and the fifteen minutes of paranoia each hour could turn into forty-five, or worse sixty.

Still, I believed I had the right to be free from my incessant worrying, asthma attacks, neurosis and paranoia. There had to be a trick to finding personal confidence.

I experimented with method exercises I'd learned in my acting classes. For instance, if I had to cry on *Y&R*, I might have recalled the guinea pig incident. I could reexperience the emotion I had with my guinea pig by repeating words aloud to myself, like "patio...cardboard box...black fur...little teeth...tight eyes." If that didn't bring the memory to life, I might amplify the sound of my beloved pet squeaking a hundred times louder than he did, or imagine little screams flying all around me and even *into* my skin. I could remember the feeling of him in my childhood hands, and stretch the sensation of his fur up my arms. Because of my fervent imagination and willingness to trick myself, method exercises worked well for me; at least they'd worked on the *Y&R* set.

However, these exercises never worked at an audition.

I imagined the audition happening in a "safe place," like my bathtub. I felt the warm water around me, heard my favorite Billy Joel song, but my hands still trembled and shook the script.

Hypnosis didn't work either.

Drinking alcohol didn't work.

I tried everything from wearing "power colors," to subconsciously "blessing" the casting person, to pinching myself out of their view in an attempt to "break the pattern of unwanted behavior." I even tried ridiculous tricks like putting cold pennies in my underwear in an attempt to distract my mind from my heavy thoughts.

Didn't work.

I tried to imagine the casting person as my friend Bruce, or my long-time, Wisconsin, friend Jamie, or Big Dog, or Mom.

Didn't work.

But what if I imagined myself as someone different? I had some success pretending to be the prison guard and holding back my real emotion with Troy.

What if I were Gregg? Or a character like Gregg? I cut out magazine pictures of a man who exuded Gregg-like confidence. I named the freckle-faced neighborhood charmer with a grin "Billy." This new character was my height and reeked of sex. I was more confident at the audition, but I didn't get the part. This new Billy I created didn't really come across as a professional actor.

So I needed to create another personality.

I cut out eight magazine pictures of men that projected professional actor confidence. I called them by one name: "Arrow," and my goal was to be their composite. The biggest photo of Arrow was a muscular blond man with an action hero's expression on his face, sitting nude on a window ledge for all to see. Other photos resembled me when I was dressed as Phillip Chancellor III at photo shoots. Another Arrow was a man in a suit and tie sitting in a director's chair, surrounded by several women stylists. I invented the back-story of Arrow to have no drama and no family dysfunction. In other words, there was nothing to keep him awake with anxiety at night. Before bed, at times, I concentrated on a photo of Arrow sleeping, and more than once this visualization *did* put me to sleep. And my auditions improved slightly when I was Arrow.

If I needed a girl to get a sexual vibe from me at an audition, I would become "Van." This persona was worldly, about 30, five-foot-ten, and a straight porn star.

I remembered that the people who showed up for my personal appearances years ago expected me to be studly, extroverted, and confident. I found the same look projected by a calendar pin-up surfer dude with an easy smile. I called him "Zane" and added him to my arsenal of personalities. Five of the nine Zane photos from magazines were of happy-go-lucky male models in Speedos.

"Jake" became the alter ego I would call on most, such as when my straight neighbor was walking his dog and I was on the spot for small-talk. Heterosexual Jake was muscular and at least two inches taller than me. He was a 25-year-old-brunette with deep, soulful eyes and beard scruff. One photo showed his wide jaw kissing a woman. Two other images were comic book illustrations of a chiseled specimen of a man in leather jacket.

One night, I parked my car and had to walk through an alley housing a gang. Afterwards I invented "Joey." He was 17 and enormous, probably six-foot-five. All brawn, no brain.

"Matthew" was who I was with Troy: an old-fashioned nature boy with horses. One photo showed him covered in gold paint in a crucifix pose. He was loving and forgiving, like Jesus.

If Big Dog and I went out to gay restaurants, I would first concentrate on photos of "TJ." This high-energy dude was young and cocky and exactly who I appeared to be when I used to bartend at gay bars. His smile told you he knew he was good-looking and not to touch.

When the novelty of sex with Big Dog started to wear off, I became "Mike Montana." Eight photos showed gay couples in tender, romantic, monogamous moments. If I was tempted to have sex with other men, or rather, leave Big Dog to have sex with other men – as I have never and would never cheat on any boyfriend – becoming Mike Montana would hopefully guarantee my fidelity and devotion to my partner. My intentions were always to stay with the partner I was with, but I have never pledged that. I've never said "I will want to be with you always," because I never wanted to hurt a man like my dad hurt Mom, when he said those things to her, then left. So I have never said those things.

Much as I'd begun to dissect my family to understand it, I'd also begun to dissect myself to understand me, hoping to rebuild a better me. Other "personalities" I formed, or discovered within myself, were two writers: one older and experienced, and the other a daring college boy. Still, other personas included the mother-part of me (her smile and look of disappointment that I'd recognize in my mirror), the father in me (patient and dominant), the little "Tommy" boy in me (guilty, victimized), the relentless overachiever (I called him "Manic"), the disciplinarian ("The Nazi," maybe modeled after my mother at her most strict), and the spiritual side of me that continually strived to be above my earthly drama (I called him "Day-in").

I did not tell anyone, not even Big Dog, that I was checking out books on multiple personalities from the Beverly Hills Library. I even used a fake ID, paranoid that if a tabloid got hold of this info, the industry would label me as crazy and unemployable.

In reading about multiples, researching how to become one for my benefit, I couldn't help but remember my mother discovering Troy's book on schizophrenia and wondering if he was schizophrenic or learning how to fake it? The multiple personality books were fascinating reading, inspiring to me, and gave me even more ideas for personalities.

I created "Edie" to keep track on an imagined computer database of every character's switching in and out. "The Monitor" would speak to everyone on a loudspeaker. I imagined a soothing, low baritone speaking to me before auditions: "Thom, we will now send in Arrow. Arrow will wake up from a nap when we call him. He is asleep on the beach of the island he and his family own in the South Pacific."

In total I created twenty-five distinct personalities. And since I was obviously feeling fragmented, and not as strong and healthy as I could be, I figured a doctor would be a nice addition to the group. In a magazine ad, I found a photo of a group of fifteen MDs and adopted them into my personality file. This group, I declared, would metaphysically heal the other characters if needed.

In case anyone found my envelope, I had written across it, "If one is overloaded trying to accomplish so much – perhaps a separation should take place. Can a group accomplish more than one?" At the bottom I wrote, "An acting exercise."

It *had* just started out as an exercise.

35

A New Name

Gregg always got more excited than I did when one of my TV shows aired. I was unhappy with my performances and thought my nerves showed onscreen, but he would brag about me to his Hollywood contacts. To him, this meant I was pursuing acting full-time and had given up the screenplay idea. Gregg warned me he'd sue if I continued writing about our family. Honoring my mother, and honoring my own path, I insisted on writing it. To placate him, I agreed to legally change my name and never refer to the name "Bierdz" in the script.

I admired a book titled *Mutant Message Down Under* about a tribe of aborigines in the Australian outback who regularly changed their names. One might go from being "food-finder" to "sleep-talker" to "sun-healer" to "music-maker."

Since "The Monitor" would look strange on my driver's license, the new name I eventually came up with was "Zoey Drake." Big Dog and Zoey sounded like the name of a cartoon, but I was used to being amused at myself by this point.

There is a freedom in having a new name, and it is relatively easy to change legally, requiring only three-hundred-dollars and sporadic visits to City Hall.

Reuniting with Troy freed me of much internal anguish, and my new identity freed me even further. My paintings began reflecting my spirit's liberation.

I couldn't have imagined I would earn my living as a painter in less than a decade. At this time, I painted each day to "zone out," but my continuous dripping of paint on Big Dog's furniture and white carpet didn't help *him* "zone out."

Since Big Dog's only hobby besides golf was a clean house, I tried his patience. Nevertheless, he was a good sport about it. Living together for almost three years made it apparent how independent we both were. Although Big Dog was a perfect mate, I grew paranoid of a continued relationship, or more so, paranoid that I would be trapped and suffocated down the line, and therefore I felt constricted by his enormous love and devotion to me.

"FREED HORSE"
(In the collection of Claire & David Tunkl)

Intoxicated by the idea of my newfound freedom relating to Troy, I moved into a very small apartment of my own in Hollywood. It made sense that I was alone again to think about what had happened over the past year – to digest it, cocoon, and then emerge, I hoped, as a bigger, better, healthier me (or Jake or Billy, etc).

Perhaps I left Big Dog because, like my father, I just needed "space."

Wishing to share this space with my newfound baby brother, I called Dr. Green every couple of weeks to check on Troy's behavior. She said he was regressing and speaking in scattered phrases.

The thought he was suffering, in any way, ate at me everyday.

Like many people in their 30s, I was taken aback discovering new feelings, or rediscovering old ones. I had spent the first half of my life in a journey trying to separate myself from my family, to become my own person. And, like a million other Americans, I was spending the second half of my life coming to grips with the realization I'd always held my family close to my heart, and I'd always need to.

That June, I used my frequent-flyer miles to visit Troy. I was shocked to see his face covered with pimples.

After I told him about my name change, leaving out the reason for it, he mumbled that he wanted a new name too. He decided on "Kiler." I told him it sounded great. Then he spelled it for me, and I realized that it was one letter away from "killer." When I pointed this out, he grinned. It turned my stomach. I refused to call him Kiler, but he nevertheless addressed me as Zoey.

He asked me if he was going to be executed. That's what the voices in his head told him. They also told him he'd be going home with a foster family. I told Troy not to believe the voices; that I'd rather he asked me his concerns, and I promised to be truthful. Troy seemed to hear my words, but he didn't register what I said. Other voices were confusing him.

During that weeklong visit, I began asking him the heavy questions. I wanted to force him, or trick him, into an apology for what he did.

"I'm not sorry I did it," he announced, pensive. "I...no, I'm not sorry." He studied my reaction, then asked me, "You'll keep coming if I'm not sorry?"

"I will keep coming," I said, "as long as you keep being honest. That is the best thing we have, I think. Most people don't have that. Let's just be honest, okay?"

He shook my hand on it.

Later, Dr. Green told me matricide perpetrators are often confused about their feelings. They might not really mean the things they say. She also stated just because Troy appeared like he wasn't remorseful, didn't mean he wasn't. She believed he was still piecing things together.

Troy and I spent much of our time together drawing. I drew houseboats on turbulent waves. He drew mostly unfinished kites in uncluttered skies. They indicated a new freedom he felt; a freedom he didn't feel when our mother was alive.

Our father decided it was time he saw Troy, and joined me one day during this trip. Our concerned father, intent on figuring out if Troy was pulling the wool over my eyes, looked helpless in the prison visiting room. He embraced Troy, but his eyes were saying: "You can't feel, can you? You are a sociopath, aren't you? When are you going to stop faking?"

Troy said our father looked "the same." Dad turned away, blinking back tears. He went to the vending machine to get Troy a candy bar of his choice. After returning, he brought up, in the least confrontational manner, the idea that perhaps Troy was faking. The visit then became tense. Troy seemed to retreat into his own world, becoming angry, and eventually retaliating with, "I'm going to Hell, but so are you for being late on child support. And all fags like Tommy go to Hell."

"Zoey is my name," I corrected him.

"Mom went to Hell because she said 'Goddamnit!'" Troy insisted, rising.

Our father said, "Let's all calm down here. Troy, come on. Sit down, please."

"Dad," I said, "don't you lecture him."

Our father repeated softly, "Sit down, Troy."

I said, "If he wants to stand, he can stand. Don't tell him what to do in his own home."

Troy whispered, "Gregg's going to Hell because he screwed all the neighborhood girls. And Hope...I don't know why, but she's going to Hell."

"Sit down," Dad said again.

"Look," I said, "You had nineteen years to tell him what to do. You only used four of the nineteen, in case you lost count."

"I didn't lose count," Dad said.

"Zo, if you want to kill yourself," Troy said, "I'll do it, too, so we can be together."

Nancy, the motherly guard, approached us.

I asked her, "Will you tell Mike or Dr. Green I need to talk to them about Troy's medication?"

Our father offered guiltily, "In the meantime, I'll go get my sons another candy bar."

I grabbed Dad's arm. "No. Troy and I get jittery if we have too much sugar."

I pointed to Troy's chair and Troy sat down. Nancy moved away.

Troy said, "Can Dad get me popcorn?"

"Only if you watch the salt," I reminded him.

"Half a packet?"

"That's right."

Our father said, "One Kit Kat's not going to make Troy jittery. How often do I get to visit here?"

"Dad, it's 12:30. We're here with Troy until 4:00. He can have candy at 1:00 and 3:00, and anything healthy in-between."

Dad argued, "I think you're being a bit ridiculous."

"Tell Dad you want a sandwich," I demanded of Troy.

Troy nodded. Dad walked to the vending machine. I leaned back in my chair, victorious: I was the father in this situation, and I wanted to make absolutely certain everybody understood my new rules.

I had to stretch and found myself at the guard desk bookshelves where there happened to be a college book, definitely out of place, mixed in with the Bibles and Sears catalogues. It was titled *The Brain*. Bored with *The Little Mermaid*, I skimmed through the book back at my seat. Troy watched me, and our father watched him.

We paged through chapters on the left and right hemispheres of the brain, and on the various cerebral functions. The pages comparing the brain to computer technology fascinated me, and interested Troy as well.

We took turns slowly reading aloud, and I'd point to the appropriate illustration or photograph. We paused for more vending machine coffee, then skimmed through Freud's theories. Troy asked for something sweet. After I checked the clock, I fetched him a small vending machine donut and we resumed our leisurely stroll through the cerebellum.

Turning a page, I collided with a chapter on schizophrenia. My tired eyes became wildly, instantly alert. I'd never read about schizophrenia, though others in my family had. Since my mother's murder, Aunt Mary had investigated as many publications on paranoid schizophrenia as I had on life-after-death.

I glanced sideways to check if Troy were daydreaming, so I could peek at the page. To my surprise, he was already reading. As my head turned to catch up with my eyes, he said, "I'm a paranoid schizophrenic, did you know that?"

Our father looked unsure.

At a loss for words, I exhaled a sigh. I still did not have enough information about whether or not he was, and I didn't want to restrict or limit him, or hurt his feelings.

"How do you know that for a fact?" I asked, discreetly closing the book.

He gently took the book from my hands and brought it close to his face. Undeterred, he opened it and relocated the chapter on schizophrenia. He began reading aloud, slowly, methodically.

"The majority of patients in mental hospitals and institutions are being treated for mood disorders, which include manic depression and chronic depression, or schizophrenia. The word schizophrenia literally means 'fragmenting of personality.'"

What I didn't want to do was place more importance on the book by taking it away from Troy. As imperceptibly as possible, I tried to stay a line ahead of his reading, preparing myself for whatever was coming next.

Struggling with the bigger words, Troy read on, "Existing in an emotionally insulated state, the schizophrenic may be aware of the outside world, but he is not 'living' in it. He is indifferent to the world the rest of us live in, and withdrawn."

"Sounds like me," I joked to make him feel better.

"The schizophrenic is confused and in disarray. Difficulty discerning what is relevant or difficulty in grasping concepts and generalizing are symptoms of the disease. He may repeat certain words or phrases or use a private logic or a language only he understands. There are cases where the schizophrenic literally becomes mute. The speech and behavior of the schizophrenic are often quite senseless to the people who observe him. The schizophrenic may suddenly shout 'Put the gun down!' when no one is yielding a gun of any sort or spend all day talking on an imaginary phone. But if symptoms are not severe, a schizophrenic may not be recognized as such by his friends, co-workers, or family. He may even be able to perform productive work, concealing to others what a difficult effort or stress level he is facing."

Troy concentrated hard on the words he read. I concentrated on Troy, watching him store this knowledge in his brain. He obviously did not remember any of the information from the schizophrenia book he read as a teenager. He was "re-experiencing" this for the first time. He continued, "The paranoid schizophrenic presents the classic symptoms of insanity. His 'mad' behavior which makes no sense to others has a secret reason behind it, for he suffers from delusions of grandeur, persecution, or even at times eroticism. He may believe that a voice from outside of his being is speaking his thoughts, or feel his actions are forced upon him by some external force. In severe situations the delusion may grow until he imagines himself the center of a government conspiracy involving terrorism, or he may imagine he is in possession of treasured religious documents, or perhaps fleeing from the Communist Party. Strangers are possible threats, and spies, and those closest to him are also suspect. He may believe his thoughts are being controlled by waves from a noisy microwave oven or he may attribute his worldwide importance to the fact that he is Jesus Christ."

Fuck, I thought. That's me.

Not only was one of my "personalities" a Jesus figure, but I also believed I had been sent on a mission to save Troy's soul.

"NOT EASY TO BE JESUS"

36

Horton Hears A Who

June 1994

T roy read on, "Paranoids may go from withdrawal to aggression in ten seconds and an unlucky stranger may be the unwitting target of his violence."

Mentally taxed, he yawned. I took this opportunity to suggest we read *The Little Mermaid*. He asked me to read not *The Little Mermaid*, but the book in his hands.

Reluctantly, curiously, I began, "The causes of these mental diseases constitute the single most important question facing psychiatry. Many studies have been done, linking schizophrenia to marijuana..."

Troy grinned, having been a marijuana user.

I continued, "Psychiatrists have switched their focus from environmental explanations to biological ones. Studies have traced the occurrence of schizophrenia within families. If the disease is genetic, then people related to a schizophrenic have a higher chance of being schizophrenic."

"Maybe you're one, too," Troy said, studying me.

I cast my eyes to my therapist father. Was he studying me also, wondering if I was schizophrenic?

Or...was I just being paranoid?

I read on, "Since at least one person in a hundred is schizophrenic, this suggests that schizophrenia is in fact hereditary. Scientists cannot locate which gene, or group of genes, is responsible. None of the drugs prescribed to schizophrenics actually cures the disease; they only address the symptoms. They are worthless in improving what doctors call the residual syndrome - a lack of motivation, emotional flatness and eccentric behavior."

I stopped, took a breath, then joked, "At least I have motivation."

Troy took the book and finished, "Most schizophrenics will never lead fully normal lives."

That pertained to Troy and not me, I hoped.

I sat frozen, next to him in the big cold sterile room, feeling like a doctor dumping a fatal diagnosis on his own son.

• • •

Dad was quiet on the ride back to Kenosha to see Hope.

"His teeth were cleaner than last time," I said. "The tobacco stains are a little washed away. He washed his hair too, dresses better, shirt tucked in. Before you came in, he told me he went to the library."

"They have a library?"

"I guess so. He got to check out a car magazine."

"That's good that he gets out of his cell from time to time."

"Mike makes him go to Special Rec now," I said, "a gym thing. Sometimes they give him a soda if he runs laps."

"That's good. I thought you said he didn't have pimples?"

"Weird. He didn't last time. Like baby's skin last time. Maybe I got him to thinking too much."

"Maybe he's eating too many potato chips. That name you want to be called. What was it?"

"Zoey."

"You said it came to you in a dream?"

"Yeah."

"I wouldn't tell too many people about that. You know, like in Hollywood."

We drove for another minute before I commented, "Why?"

"Why what?"

"Keep Zoey to myself?"

"RAVAGED FACE OF SPIRIT"

"Keep the idea that you heard a voice to yourself. People won't understand."

"You have such a small mind sometimes."

"I'm not trying to hurt you."

"But you are. You're stopping me from...I don't know...good things."

"Like hearing voices?"

"There are times I can't sleep...nightmares, and I know that's normal...and Aunt Dianne has recurring nightmares...and I wish I could escape them and go someplace, and it's like another channel of my brain clicks in."

"Voices?"

"Occasionally – and I mean like four times in my whole life. Once I heard a chirping in my bedroom and thought it was a mouse. I asked my guides what it was, and a voice said, 'Usually on the ceiling.' And at first I thought – shit – the ceiling? Troy used to watch screaming bugs on the ceiling. So I was afraid to look up. But I did. And I saw a smoke detector. That was the chirping! It was low on batteries. I had no idea fire detectors chirped until that voice *told* me."

"You didn't know they made a beeping sound?"

"I didn't. There's got to be more than this, Dad, what we see everyday, I know there has to be more. So at night I ask, and try to hear things, to see things. It puts me to sleep, like I'm trying so hard to hear it, and wham, I go to sleep for a little while. But when I get up, I wonder who did I hear? Am I so studied and evolved that I am privy to the things in the brain others don't see? Or are the synapses in my brain misfiring? A few of my friends hear similar voices, and one actually believes we are living many lives at once, and there is no linear time. That the voices clue us into what is going on in our other lives."

"That is a lot to digest."

"Are there words and messages floating around us in space, only to be noticed by artists," I smiled, "and the super-sensitive? Like Dr. Seuss' *Horton Hears A Who?*"

"Where the elephant heard the little voice from tiny people living in a flower?"

"Exactly! And there was a whole village inside that flower that only the elephant could hear at first, then everybody found out about the Whos and the elephant was no longer thought of as crazy!"

"Not based on a true story, you know."

I laughed, "Yeah, I know. But it makes me wonder if people like Troy are maybe not crazy, but are more in tune in another part of their brain, like highly evolved, really sensitive people who don't know how to reign it in. Like they're blessed or something."

"Troy is not blessed."

"Why are you always limiting me?"

"The rest of the world won't believe you, Thom. You can tell me what you want, and I may even believe you, but strangers won't."

"Joan of Arc heard a voice. Mother Teresa heard God. An angel came to Edgar Cayce when he was 11 and asked him what he wanted to do with the rest of his life, and he said 'heal people,' and he did."

"You're not Edgar Cayce."

"Why limit me, Dad?"

"Your paintings look exactly like the ones in that book. Did you notice that? The ones by the schizophrenics?"

"Some of them. Yes."

I tried to hide my fear from him. Yes, I had never seen paintings more similar to mine. Yes, I had more evidence to support me being "crazy" – in my luggage I had an envelope with magazine photos of my forty personas. Who wouldn't think they were multiple personalities? I didn't even know if they were.

"If Troy, in fact, is schizophrenic," he said, "damn it...all I'm saying is you should be aware, but I don't think you are schizophrenic."

"I am aware," I said. I didn't say I was aware Troy needed me to be Matthew; and casting people needed me to be Arrow; and it was easier to pretend to be Van than to tell a flirty girl I was gay; and Hope needed me to be one of the straight characters like Jake; and Big Dog had needed me to be Mike Montana, but I had problems being Mike Montana, so I left; and when I needed to write through the entire night about Mom's struggle, I needed to be Manic.

I said, "I am aware that I, like anybody else, can become a lot more than they think is possible."

"Be careful who you share your dreams with. They may think you have delusions of grandeur."

"We really don't know that until I'm dead, because maybe I *will* do great things."

"You moved out to Hollywood to be a movie-star. That was unrealistic. But you did it. Well, a TV star."

"Seven-thousand girls packed into a mall in Toronto to see me. They wanted my autograph."

"Where are they now?"

"Toronto."

"I mean do they want your autograph anymore? This was six years ago. They mistook you for your character. They weren't there to see the real you. But they'd like the real you – they just didn't know you, Thom. TJ. Zoey."

"Maybe not the gay me. That is why I can become this other character, if I have to."

"What other character?"

"Never mind."

"Zoey?"

"Arrow."

"Who is Arrow now?"

"These photos I have. This successful actor in these photos. I try to become Arrow when I audition. It's acting."

He looked at me skeptically.

I said, "Mom would understand."

"It's time you let your mother go."

"Maybe the world is a little bigger than you think it is."

"Losing her, and then losing your shot at fame. I'm sorry, Thom."

"Zoey."

"Arrow. Whoever. I'm sorry."

I was sorry too. Sorry a sentence from *The Existential Manual* kept repeating in my head. The book defined schizophrenia as: "A special strategy that a person invents in order to live in an unlivable situation."

Shit. That was me. My secret method exercises were, indeed, a special strategy. How could I deny that?

Over supper at a truck stop, Dad tried to initiate a heart-to-heart talk about his failed dreams. He was trying to comfort me, but I had so many conversations going on inside my head that I couldn't listen to him. I decided I would rather talk to Troy. He understood me better than anyone, as unsettling as that was.

The next day, I drove to see Troy.

Maybe I hadn't seen enough of Troy, but when Troy met me in the visitation room, he had clearly seen enough of me. He was exhausted. His invisible cigarette wasn't cutting it. He needed a real one.

"Can this be our last visit?" he said, tired.

"What?"

"Can this be our last visit?"

"Oh, I'll be here tomorrow."

"But can this be our last visit?"

"You don't want to see me anymore?"

He shook his head no.

Masking my hurt, I said, "Aah...sure. If that's what you want. I'll tell you what. I'm going to find a hotel in Portage for the night. I'll come here in the morning, and if you don't want to see me, you don't have to."

He didn't acknowledge me the rest of the visit and wouldn't shake my hand goodbye.

The next day, I arrived early.

Mike appeared. Troy didn't want to see me anymore. Mike told me Troy was a different person every day. Troy was sometimes paranoid, sometimes content. Sometimes he missed me; sometimes he refused to accept my daily postcards.

Along with optimistic words, I wrote Troy that I understood I'd over-stayed my welcome, and that I loved him no matter what – loved him un-conditionally. At the time, I believed I did love Troy unconditionally. But I did not – could not – really love him unconditionally, until the matter of the night of my mother's murder was resolved.

Finishing the card, I wrote a suggestion that he phone me, so we could talk about Gregg's elaborate wedding to Patsy, which was sched-uled the following week.

He didn't call.

37

The Same Voice

1994

Ironically, cell phones can be used anywhere but in a cell. Inmates have to use a public phone in a common area. It's impossible for someone outside prison to phone someone inside a prison, so I wrote to Troy asking him to phone me. I asked Mike to assist him in doing so.

Troy finally called one autumn afternoon when Gregg was visiting my apartment and proudly showing off his honeymoon pictures from France, and giving me expensive Parisian shirts Patsy bought for me.

I held the phone, wanting to hear Troy's remorse at last. That is not what I heard.

"Zo, when I see her in Heaven she'll beat me up," he said.

"Mom doesn't have it in her to beat you or anybody up."

"That's what's going to happen. I'm telling you. I know. I'll go up on a cloud and Mom'll come after me. She'll tell the angels I'm the one that killed her. She'll point and scream and carry on and send me to Hell."

"There's no reason for somebody as loving as God to make Hell. He doesn't want to punish you or anyone. He's so far beyond our greatest expectations that we can't fathom his understanding, unconditional love, and compassion. To judge and to want to beat someone up are human traits. He's not like that. And you know Mom – she's not like that either."

"She's angry I killed her."

"Your conscience is convincing you of that, but when Mom was alive did she ever try to hurt you?"

"No, but I never killed her before."

"But you used to hurt her. She never hurt back, right?"

"I don't want to talk about this with you."

"Okay," I said, "see, Troy, we grew up Catholic and we were taught to fear God."

"But the Bible says–"

"I've been learning some things about the Bible. It was changed by men in power, Troy. Politicians. This is a fact. I heard it on the news. The Bible says some really good things about holy stuff like miracles and love, but the references to fear and judgment were added by men, so they could run their society the way they wanted. This is how it is – Mom doesn't hate you – Mom loves you."

"Why?"

"Because you're family."

I was deliberately looking Gregg in the eye when I said this, to reiterate that he and Troy were also family, and could be reunited in that sense. But if Gregg was feeling any sentiment at all, he hid it.

Troy went on to tell me the reason there were clouds in Heaven was to cover your private parts when you went to the bathroom.

Troy spoke about masturbation, and how dirty it was. And how he was worried our mother could watch him.

I said, "If Mom sees you masturbate, she knows more now. We're in a physical world with physical opportunities and challenges, but Mom is beyond that now. She's more open-minded than she used to be. We have to forget what the angry nuns told us. Mom sees we are still down here learning Earth lessons. We have physical bodies on Earth. Masturbation is a physical exercise. Our bodies are not sinful. That doesn't make sense, does it? If they were sinful, it would be like entrapment or something."

Gregg collected his photos and went home to Patsy. He was uncomfortable with our discussion of masturbation.

• • •

My father and I were talking over the phone more openly, and more

193

regularly, about a variety of topics. He read some spiritual books that I suggested to him. He loved these and recommended other ones with similar themes for me to read. I never would have guessed we'd have so much in common.

· · ·

It wasn't long before I landed another acting job, once again playing a murderer, on Aaron Spelling's short-lived *Robin's Hoods*. Bombshells played ex-cons turned into crime-fighters. As a guest star, I had a scene where I had to emote behind prison bars. I did this with the help of my method exercises. I was looking out, my hands grasping the cold steel, begging for someone to understand and believe in my innocence. I was again playing Troy.

Filming *Robin's Hoods* was great – nine days at a four-star hotel in Vancouver. I didn't worry about my apartment or plants, as Gregg had called, out of the blue a few days prior, wanting to hide out at my place. He and Patsy were already quarreling over her abandonment issues. Gregg claimed she had threatened him with physical harm.

When I returned, Gregg picked me up at the airport. His eyes were red from crying, I guessed.

I asked him, "Is it Patsy?"

"No. Troy called this morning," he said.

"Really?"

"Yup. The machine said it was collect from C.C.P. and I thought if I didn't pick up, he might think you were home and didn't want to talk to him. I didn't want to ruin his whole day. So I picked up."

"You talked to Troy?"

Gregg, distant, drove down the airport exit ramp.

"What'd you guys talk about?" I asked.

"I just told him you were filming in Vancouver."

"I sent him letters. He should've known I was in Canada."

"He said he got one this morning, and you have some letters from him at your apartment."

"Really? How'd he sound?"

"The same. He sounds just like you. And me. We all have the same voice."

Gregg went off on a tangent about fate. About how if he hadn't been staying at my apartment, and if I hadn't gone out of town, and if he hadn't been there that Friday morning, he would never have talked to Troy.

Gregg told me he'd started to believe that everything in our lives was fated. Even his hair falling out in chunks. That it was senseless to believe, as I did, that we could alter our destinies.

I hated hearing this. My life had been full of anxiety, and I did not want it to be destined to continue like that.

"What about your marriage to Patsy? You say every other day you want to get out. Is it fate or free will?"

"I'll move back in with her when she cools down. She was right when she said she knew we were supposed to be soul mates."

"You don't sound convinced."

"Last month, she and I went to the Hearst Castle, and I looked at my Spanish beauty across the famous pool, with all those sculptures, and the way she looked at me – I knew it was perfect. She's gorgeous, and I'm lucky to have someone who loves me so much, and all she wants to do is take care of me. We'll even have kids that go to Pepperdine with stars' kids."

He changed the subject, "And I was fated to hear Troy's voice one last time. That's why you got the job in Canada."

"One last time?"

"Troy's not going to last long."

"I don't know."

"Don't look so smug," Gregg said. "It doesn't mean anything."

"What doesn't?"

"That I talked to him. He still killed her."

"Maybe you'd like to write him a note. Just say 'hi.' So he can keep it in his room and think of you."

Blood rushed into Gregg's face, "Why would I want him to think of me at all?"

"You taught him how to dribble a basketball."

"I wish he had killed himself a long time ago. Then none of this would've happened. Don't you wish he would've killed himself instead?"

Oddly, as much as I loved Troy, if I had to choose losing him or Mom, I would pick Troy dying. I'd prefer someone kill himself, over someone being victim to another's actions.

But Troy was not dead. Whether Gregg was right about Troy's life expectancy being short, I didn't know. I only knew both my brothers were alive, and they communicated on this particular day.

This would never happen again.

38

Unexpected Words

1994

I was torn apart by Troy's letters. And elated as well.

Letters From Troy

...i wasnt fealing rite about you visiting me. my life REALLY got out of control for a while their! i miss you being my brother while im free. **do you miss the free life w/me?** *tell me. let me know. your still my older brother ...*

...mary mother of god. The priest thought i was robin hood, yes that's the truth. he told me if i killed some body i could be a priest in heven. and that i could be married. because you know priests normally can't be married. did you know you have to pray a rosary in order to go to hell? im lazy and i like to watch the day go by.

i have blood on my teeth. stains. one time i read the Charlie Manson murders book. it had my name in the book it said and this is the truth that i was one of the gang and that i had to run the squads. or it was something close to that

i should rite something about the pigs it would be famous writting. **do you save my letter in case i could never write to you again** *or do you just read them once. how attached to me are you really. here is a ballon i had!* (He had sketched a heart balloon) *it was with print and from a girlfriend*

"CONFLICTED DEMON / ANGEL BOY"

of mine i forgot all about until now, funny how some times you just meat people and they seem to think they have the rite.

you dont have to worrie im just in the system now. i have never said i love you to you or anyone elts. *do you get angry at me behind my back?* **do you get stuck in life ever?** *is it like other peoples problems? i think im better than you! im a good kid i meant! do you know when you like people? you treat people well? i find my self w/well frome dads writtings. are you w/enough money?*

hav i left you w/enuff fealings? *are your fealing hurt when i make mistakes when i write to you? Are you sure we go to heven when we both die? because il have alot of questions for you by then. do you miss anything? do you think they could have given you more of something? could you be more normal?* **do you wish somehow that you could be normal again?** (Troy drew pictures of a kite and, across from it, lightning over storm clouds)

do you think mom was a murder a gang murder and mabey i was trying to get some respect. for my colors? do i still go to heaven? *write back. im wondering if you and gregg will forget me when we all die.*

i think mabey i killed mom for gregg, *i like gregg i like to have his attention our times together are like golden to me more than special. mom made heaven look good to me she said nothing but i though it was so good that it just didnt deserve mom. i wanted to spend time with mom to. we just couldn't spend any real time together,* **she didnt deserve to have boyfriends that would keep her apart from me**

you do know im a parinoid schizophrenic dont you. now you know. i have schizophrenia. it means im afraid of people.
love troy

My father pointed out that Troy's use of the small "i" when referring to himself showed his low sense of self-worth. The only name he considered important enough to capitalize was Charlie Manson. To Troy, Manson deserved to be capitalized, but "Mary, Mother of God" did not.

There came even more letters:

zo, when we die, do we have wings or halows. do the angels have halows? or do they have wings? just a question. what do we look like in heaven again i forgot. Write me and tell me please, i will call you soon after i get your letter. im doing good.

im just worried a little about suicide latter on in life. *i was wondering what the commandments ment exactly. i was wondering if you broke a commandment if that ment you were to go to hell exactly...*

...i don't know if i can face what i did. if i go to hell you will come for me wont you?...*why did i kill my mother?...i must have mistaken mom for caeser my pit bull.*

...will you have a chance to steal me away from satin? *are you and gregg going to fight him off for me.*

*i think its time we decided to become a family again without mom. just me you and gregg we could do it all if we had the chance...**your being too polite with me i want the answers.***

i heard a voice of you saying thats what brothers are for going to hell for you? **i hear voices all of the time i just pick one.**

i cant help but thinking if i would have only killed my self first? **mom came to me as an angel in my room.**

...dont you think brothers should be tourchered together? *...ill kill myself. i will go buy a gun rite now!! and if you die i will die to so we can be together rite away.*

With the Last of My Love Because i Will go to Hell Unless their is love left
Your brother troy

His suicide-talk scared me. I realized for certain I did not want him to die. But there was no way for me to get hold of him. I would have to wait for him to call me.

One October morning, the phone rang at 5:30 AM.

"I've been mean my entire life, Zo," Troy blurted.

He had never stood back and pragmatically assessed his life. I wanted to say "No, you haven't," but in fact I couldn't remember anything he'd done that wasn't done out of meanness, out of fear. Later, I remembered him building furniture with me, and him fiddling with a guitar. I regretted not sharing those memories.

He explained he had only hurt things and he had never done anything good. Trying to be encouraging, I told him it wasn't too late, he could do good things now – that we had free will.

But he started to speak in a panic about his past.

Most of that phone call consisted of Troy talking about feeling guilty for cheating on his five girlfriends. This made no sense to me, but it made sense to Troy. He categorically announced he had dated five girls and he was going to go to Hell because he had cheated on them.

Troy believed, from his narcissistic perspective, the world outside had not changed. He believed the five girls he dated were still sitting around all day, thinking about him, and growing more furious all the time.

"Don't worry about that," I advised. "Think about now and the future. What are you going to do today? What did you have for breakfast?"

"I shouldn't have been so mean, Zo," he said, "I killed Mom."

He'd never spoken those words of remorse to me before. He'd written about our mother, but for different reasons. Then he was reacting from fear – fear of Hell. But at this moment, his tone of voice didn't carry fear. He was speaking from his heart.

"Do you regret that?" I asked very matter-of-factly, as a therapist would.

"Of course I do, Zo, you know that," he said, as reasonably and matter-of-factly as I had.

My brother was climbing the ladder of recovery. He was feeling remorse, and he was aware of it. This was a necessary and important step in his evolution. He was being reasonable, and he spoke like a reformed convict, accepting the consequences of his actions. He had come full-circle. Less than a year after my reaching out to him, he was remorseful.

· · ·

Family values.

Since the 1980s, starting with the Reagan revolution, our politicians have made a big show about setting up political action committees and academic departments focused on "preserving" the American family. Groups like the "Family Research Council," the "Center for Marriage and Family Studies," "Focus on the Family," and the "American Family Association" were created to protect the American family from outside forces. But do any of these groups understand that what shatters a family really comes from inside of it?

There's a reason why politicians are reluctant to turn over the rock of the American family: they're afraid of what they'll find under it. From time to time, we enjoy the spectacle of the governor discovered with a hooker, or the priest coming out of a gay bar, or the schoolteacher caught on *Dateline* seducing minors over the internet. In the corresponding newspaper stories, the headline is sensational, and naughtily sexy, but the first paragraph will tell you what "a good father and family man" he is, or what a "devoted wife and churchgoer" she is.

And so while the sanctity of marriage and family provides a convenient excuse for political posturing, its secrets remain largely under wraps, where most politicians – not to mention most families – would prefer they stay.

"HANDICAPPED BROTHERS"
(In the collection of Joe Argazzi)

39

Christmas Delusions

FRIENDSHIP
A friend is a person who stands by you,
not careing what the rest will do.
– TROY BIERDZ

December 23 to 25, 1994

For the first Christmas in many years, I didn't have a boyfriend or other commitment, and I wanted to spend the holidays with Troy.

But would Troy change his mind again? Would he not want to see me? Did he have another mood swing since our recent phone call? Would he come out to the visiting room and greet me with a polite, "Can this be our last visit?"

As it turned out, he was thrilled to see me. Though he was a little uncomfortable being out of his regular schedule – this being the first time in six months he'd ventured away from his routine and had a visitor. His eyes perused the room with apprehension. We shook hands and sat down.

I had a few days of beard scruff. He commented on it.

He had gained weight. It showed mostly on his face, but he also had a little potbelly. His skin had fewer blemishes. His hair was long and unkempt. His beard was months old and scraggly. His thick mustache reminded me of the ones I saw in old westerns.

He looked "good, like a rustic cowboy," I told him, "I can't grow a mustache that thick and long." He smiled for a second, proud of his masculinity. But another topic was pressing on his mind.

"I have five girlfriends and I cheated on them. I'm going to Hell. They'll send me to Hell."

"When did you have the girlfriends?"

He thought about it. He stared at my left shoe resting on my right knee. We were sitting deliberately close, bent over, because he didn't want the other visitors to eavesdrop.

I continued, "That was over five years ago. Have you had the girlfriends since?" I knew he hadn't, but I wanted to see if he knew he hadn't.

"They're still my girlfriends," he insisted.

"You haven't seen them while you were here at C.C.P., have you?"

"No."

"Well, I think," I said as gently as possible, "they have probably moved on."

It didn't register. He concentrated on my shoe. He stuck out his index finger and tapped my sole. He glanced up to gauge my reaction. I didn't give him one.

He tapped the sole of my shoe again, continuing at a steady beat as he rocked in his chair. He was totally focused on his tapping, as was I. I was frozen in surprise, but extremely touched by his gesture. So taken aback, in fact, that my stream of consciousness deserted me. He continued for a long while. He glanced at the security guards to check if tapping were in violation of the rules. From the corner of my eye, I caught them looking curiously at us. They weren't sure if shoe tapping was allowed. I felt they were mildly embarrassed for me, or…was I being paranoid? In the meantime, I blurted out some sort of conversation to hide my discomfort. I wasn't used to reaching out in a physical way. Neither was Troy.

I rattled on about the fight he'd gotten into in the cafeteria the prior week. The guards at Admittance informed me Troy had been put under surveillance and temporarily locked up. Troy didn't want to talk about it.

He stopped tapping my foot. He glanced up at me for my reaction. I nodded to him.

"This touching – you and me – it wouldn't happen before, on the outside, would it?" he asked.

Once, when he was a teenager and we were at our father's apartment, Troy broke down in tears at the supper table. He ran upstairs, and I ran after him, forcing a hug on him. Though he resisted, I held on, trying to lessen his pain. He pushed me away.

"No," I answered him, "Probably not."

"Kinda strange, don't you think?" he rambled, "The whole thing. The shoe and all. That here I am in prison."

I nodded. After awhile I changed the subject. "Gregg got back with his wife," I said.

"I know. You told me."

"Well, you never said anything."

"What am I supposed to say? He's a grown man."

"I found out today he and Patsy are pregnant."

"She is?"

"I can't believe they're rushing into this, but Patsy feels she has one egg left to drop or something."

"He's gonna be a dad."

"Right. Did you want to ask about anybody else?"

"Do you know David Hasselhoff? *Entertainment Tonight* says he used to be on *The Young and the Restless*."

"I meant like Hope."

"Why doesn't she have any kids?"

I'd promised Hope that I wouldn't tell Troy she had a daughter, and was pregnant with another, so I changed the subject, "Dad's okay."

"Dad?"

"Yeah."

"He shouldn't have divorced. That'll get him in Hell, Zo."

"He loves us, you know."

Troy shrugged.

"I think he always did," I said.

"Why didn't he see us more when we were small?"

"Mom scared him away."

He grinned. I didn't know why. We bought pretzels and played Uno. I remembered us playing when I visited in January, and how disoriented he was then. I used to let him win. I didn't have to do that anymore. My little brother could hold his own at Uno now.

After a couple more games and coffees, he was jittery and no longer wanted to play. My suggestion was to draw a "Happy New Year" card to Gregg and Patsy, and one to Big Dog, whom I still saw weekly as a friend. We shared a pencil, passing it back and forth until the drawings were complete. They were a combination of my primitive, whimsical style and his abstract style. I signed – *Love, Zo* – on the cards. I suggested Troy sign the cards also. He wrote – *love, troy*. Afterward he fidgeted nervously and kept rereading the cards. Sometime later, he crossed out the word "love" by his name, and was then able to relax.

Even though I was concerned about Troy's health and watched his sugar intake, there was nothing I could do to get him to quit smoking. Troy had few pleasures, so I bought him cigarettes from the vending machine. The inmates were allowed to take two packs back with them. Troy snatched them greedily; reminding me of the way Abu would snatch his monkey biscuits. Troy pocketed the Winstons. From time to time during our visit, he glanced down to check them and excitedly finger the plastic wrappings.

The visit ended, and Troy again asked me to save him from going to Hell. I told him not to worry about that.

But Troy was stuck.

• • •

That particular Christmas Eve I spent at Aunt Mary's, along with Hope's family, and our grandparents. Next to her multi-colored tree, I had a chance to talk man-to-man with my grandfather. I was curious about the mindset of this five-foot-tall man who never talked about himself, curious for selfish reasons – how much did he influence who I was?

When I told Grandpa he looked healthy enough to live to be 110, he smiled, closed his yellow eyes, and confessed he didn't want to be around that long.

"You going to expound on that?" I invited.

"No." Like a turtle he dropped his head into his body.

"Mom was like that. She didn't tell us what was really going on with her," I chided.

I meant it as a bad thing, a less-than-healthy thing. He took it as a compliment.

"She was like me," he smiled.

"But don't you think...she could have had things...easier?"

"Life isn't easy."

I remembered him saying that over and over again when I was a child. And I remembered him always having a very challenging workload. I wondered to what extent his statement became a self-fulfilling prophecy. And how many of his learned thought-patterns were passed on to his children and grandchildren.

Christmas is a constant reminder that patterns are passed down from generation to generation.

My mother always had blue Christmas tree lights. The tree was real with long bushy needles, and the lights were the big outdoor style, emitting a serene blue glow. Since her death, I've kept the tradition of a blue-lit tree alive any year I've celebrated Christmas in my own home.

• • •

On Christmas Day, I visited Troy again. He was anxious.

"I thought you circled the 24th on the reindeer postcard you sent," he said, "I waited all day yesterday."

"Aah, no," I said, "I circled the 23rd and the 25th. You look good in short hair."

"SEPIA THOUGHT PATTERNS"

His mangled mane had been cut into a clean flattop, similar to mine. "And you shaved," I stopped. He had shaved – half his face.

"You forgot to shave your left side," I noted.

He wasn't listening, and didn't seem to mind only half of his face was shaven.

"I'm going to Hell," he said.

This seemed a good time to change the subject. I reported that certain members of the family asked about how he was doing. I related how much they had grown, and that cousin Paul had married a girl who already had a child. I told him that I'd done some research and had discovered that the bar, Rascals, he used to frequent, had burned down. Underscoring this with, "See, Troy, people move on. It's not like it was five years ago. People aren't sitting at home thinking about you all the time."

He said, "My girlfriends are."

"No, they aren't. I found out that Brenda is pregnant with another man's baby. I couldn't find the other four names you gave me."

Dejected, Troy gathered the Uno cards and dealt us each a hand. We played four games in almost complete silence. Later, as we sat back, I asked him if he'd received his Christmas gifts.

He informed me he had. He'd received the plastic bag of potato chips, frozen apple juice, and two homemade cookies that each inmate is given at Christmas. And he was grateful.

That's not what I was referring to. I was referring to the checks my father and I had sent, for him to use for shoes or something in the Sears catalogue.

More than most children, we'd been showered with gifts – however inexpensive – at Christmas. It was inconceivable that one of us would only receive snack food for the holiday. I'd never before imagined what holidays were like for an inmate. Learning that only ten percent of inmates are ever visited, I would always wonder how the unvisited ninety percent reacted to that bag of chips, cookies, and frozen apple juice.

Troy moved his arm slowly toward me. Something was up, and I tried to follow him, without seeming to notice what he was doing.

His arm crept around the back of my chair, finally touching me. His fingers were near the back of my throat. We sat, motionless, for a long time. I, feeling the heat of his arm, and he feeling the heat of my back. The guards watched. They didn't comment, but after a while Troy retracted his arm, and slowly, deliberately leaned his shoulder into mine. I didn't know if he was comparing sizes, as he often did, or just wanted to touch me again. After a while, I followed his lead and tapped his shoe, as a signal of returned affection. I only tapped once.

"The *Kenosha News*," he exclaimed, "I had Route 71, I think it's Route 71, maybe it's Route 72. Route 72 hasn't been delivered in ten years. I'm going to Hell."

"I had a paper route too," I told him. "One more thing we have in common, huh? I hated carrying the heavy, wet *Milwaukee Journals* when I was little. I lost money because my bookkeeping was off. The worst part was waking up before the sun came out."

Troy didn't believe me when I told him the *Kenosha News* would've hired his replacement years ago.

"Zo, if you love me, you have to move back to Kenosha."

"I'm not going to move back."

"But you have to."

"Why do I have to?"

"You have to move back to Kenosha and do my route."

I laughed, "Troy, I don't want to be a paperboy again."

"If you do my route then you would save me from Hell."

"I can't do that," I said.

"Why not?"

"I don't want to deliver papers in Kenosha; I want to do something a little more, uh, creative."

He looked at me, helpless.

"Troy, you don't need me to do that. Tell you what, I'll go to the *Kenosha News* and find out who is doing Route 71 or 72. Then you'll know it's been taken care of."

"Nobody's doing it! I keep telling you. I never quit!"

211

"Aah, I think your customers would've complained by now."
"No."
He picked up the pencil, "You have to bring them this."

The 72 street the 73 street and the 74 street
route number hasent been done in ten years
i lost my bags and the book. i have 72 papers.
im quitting my route i hope you can find somebody
quickly to do the route. i dont know the route
number just the streets their in Kenosha.
one day i didnt get the papers and i didnt
know who to call about it, the paper route
hasent been done since. This is my two week notice

While he had the pencil in his hand, I asked him to write out the full names and details of his other four girlfriends, in hopes that I could locate them. As he wrote, he spoke to me, like a king delegating responsibilities to his most trusted duke.

"Tell them I got mixed up with five different girls. Rhonda is the only real girlfriend. I want to break up with the others." His eyelashes were dripping as he grimly stated, "I'm never going to have children like my cousins and Gregg."

This would have occurred to other people six years ago.

"Aah," I said, "but you never wanted children anyway, right?"

"I never thought about it before."

"See? So it's no big deal."

"But I want kids now, Zo."

"No you don't."

But he did. It was all over his face. He was thinking how good it would feel to play catch with a little Troy Bierdz, Jr.

"I should be a dad," he said.

Trying to change the subject, I asked, "Have you written Dad lately?"

He thought very deeply. I watched his mind click channels. He was in his own, separate world. He let me in by sharing, "If I had the key, I'd be out by now."

I wasn't following him. "What key?" I asked.

"Mom's house key."

"What about it?"

"If I had the key, I'd be out by now."

"No, Troy, you wouldn't."

"Yes, I would. That's what they said when they arrested me. If I had the house key, I'd get out in five or ten years."

"Who said that?"

"The cops."

"I doubt they said that."

"Yes, they did."

"Troy, you got life in prison because you were unremorseful, and all of us in the family signed victim statements asking the judge to give you the steepest sentence possible."

He was hurt by the last part of that. "If I had the house key, I could go home," he insisted.

It stunned me that this made sense to him. "I told you we sold Mom's house."

He was shocked, "What? You sold it?"

"We went over this before. You and Mom were the only ones living there. And you killed Mom."

"But the house is mine. I thought the house is mine."

"Why?"

"It's my house. I thought I would get it when I get out."

I raised my eyebrows, "You're ridiculous to think you would get the house after you killed her."

"None of you guys needed it. It's for me."

"You abused her."

"I could still go there if I had a key."

"Somebody else owns that house. They don't want you there. This is your home. They treat you nice here, right?"

"Yeah," he said, resigned.

"This is your home. You have your own room. You can't go back to Mom's house. You've been here for almost six years. That's a long time."

He studied the ceiling, totally confused.

The next day, we would finally discuss our mother's murder in detail.

"OVERBURDENED MOTHER"

40

Chocolate Is Alive

December 26, 1994

From court interviews and autopsy papers, I'd become familiar with many of the details of the day my mother was murdered.

At my mother's request, John, a well-meaning cousin, picked up Troy from the halfway house, and drove him to Mom's during the afternoon of July 14, 1989. Cousin John stayed talking to Troy and Mom until about 4:30 PM. Mom was wearing a yellow long-sleeved sweater, blue jeans, and green and burlap slippers. Hope arrived a short time later. Troy asked Mom for the car keys. She said no. Troy called her a bitch. Hope had enough of our mother being called names and left. Mom walked Hope to the car. Hope asked if Mom were going to be all right. Mom said yes. Hope said she would call her later to check on her.

At about 6:00 PM, Mom drove Troy to his friend's house. She waited in the car as Troy walked to the door and asked if his friend would sell him his father's gun. Troy explained he wanted to kill his mother. The friend did not give him the gun. Mom was sitting in the car during the conversation just out of hearing range.

Mom drove Troy to another cousin's house for supper. John was there as well. After supper, they discussed religion. Troy mentioned numerology and Satan. He said someday he would snap and get revenge on the family.

At about 7:30 PM, John arranged to come to Mom's house the next morning to install cable wire. He arrived on schedule the following day. Music was playing, but no one answered the door. John went to my Grandfather DiLetti's for extra keys, and they returned to Mom's house. They went in through the patio door. Mom was on the floor, dead. Her eyes were open.

But I didn't know her last words.

• • •

I asked Troy if he remembered her last words. Did he know if she felt much pain? What was she doing in those last seconds?

He spoke fairly impersonally, explaining our mother stood up through four blows to the head. Four. I wondered if there was a correlation to her having four children.

He didn't remember her falling.

He said it wasn't premeditated. It just happened.

He said he couldn't help it. He lost control of his body.

I didn't believe him.

Maybe Troy couldn't, or wouldn't, remember the truth. Maybe the schizophrenia he'd descended into during those five years of his isolated prison sentence muddled his memory beyond recovery. Based upon the condition in which I found him, facts did not stand up against his own mind's fictions. As our conversation continued, even mundane and indisputable facts could not alter his "memories."

I asked him about the weeklong events which led up to his arrest.

"Zo, I was only gone one day."

"Troy, it was a week."

"It was only one day. I remember because I got to Dallas in only one day."

Though I tried, I couldn't convince him otherwise.

I asked him what it was like to kill a person. Was it like killing the pets he used to have?

He denied ever killing a pet.

Troy truly didn't appear to remember any portion of his detailed catalogue of animal abuse. Could he shut off his memories as easily as he shut off painful sensations? Is that how he managed to "believe" our mother's murder wasn't premeditated, even though back home I had four-hundred pages of court records equaling premeditation.

One thing Troy hadn't forgotten was the feeling of killing her, and sickened me to hear him describe it.

He grinned as he talked about the adrenalin rush he got after murdering her. I listened like a reporter, willing myself not to reveal any emotion at all. I didn't tell him to wipe the smirk off his face. But that's exactly what I wanted to say. I wanted to lecture him. I wanted to tell him he was wrong for feeling what he was feeling. It angered and shamed me that I understood his power-tripping, as I experienced it firsthand abusing Abu.

Murdering our mother was probably the most important thing Troy did in his life. Nothing else he'd done had affected so many people. It's what changed him from ordinary. It gave him a false sense of importance, provided a sense of individuality and temporary significance, and brought him national TV and tabloid coverage. It was all he had to gloat about.

He grew irritable and tired and wanted to end the visit early. That was fine with me. As much as I had tried to listen as an unbiased reporter, I was still a mama's boy who needed a few hours away from my mama's killer.

• • •

I resented Troy all that night and all the next morning. How *dare* he gloat about the murder. I was absolutely disgusted with him. But I'd agreed to be there for him *unconditionally*. And this was surely the test. Could I even stomach being next to him again?

• • •

The visiting room was crowded because it was "Bus Day." Twice a month visitors were bussed up from Milwaukee for free.

I prepped our little table with crayons and paper and playing cards, then got myself some yogurt from the vending machine.

Instead of Troy coming to greet me, Mike did. He'd just had a therapy session with Troy. Mike was concerned that Troy had been getting "stuck" in his delusions. Changing Troy's medicine had not brought about the desired effect. Mike and Dr. Green suggested Troy be transferred to another institution, a medium security facility with more resources for delusional inmates. C.C.P. wasn't a psychiatric hospital, and it wasn't set-up to treat insane men, only to cage them. I didn't like the idea of Troy leaving maximum-security. I wondered, to myself, if he could escape a less-secure institution, and it being nearer to my sister's home, I feared that she would fear for her life.

Mike, who was always generous with his time, explained that Troy, a creature of habit, did not want to leave his comfort-zone at C.C.P., even if it meant going to a place that offered more opportunities for inmates, and less restrictions. Mike asked me to talk Troy into accepting the transfer gracefully.

Instead, I asked Mike if the transfer could be avoided. Mike said yes, but only if Troy's delusions and the related anxiety decreased. Mike shook my hand and left.

Troy came out and sat by me, skittish.

We'd been assigned a front table in direct view of thirty other full tables. We were stared at, because I now knew many of the regular visitors, and they were intrigued by my former celebrity status. They stared at Troy also. Troy took in the sixty sets of eyes, then he turned quickly to me. I shrugged. He took a crayon, looked at the paper, but did not draw anything.

I didn't mind his being frustrated and paranoid. I didn't mind his suffering then, as I was still angry for his coldness of the previous day. But even with my staring at him, over the next hour, he was able to shrug off the dozens of extra eyes better than I could. He became semi-relaxed in this uncomfortable setting. It was, after all, the living room in his home. His focus became me, and me alone.

I pictured my mother's hurt as Troy, being very unemotional about it, killed her in the scenario I was then imagining. How unfair that at her last moments she didn't even feel his love – or concern – or respect. It would have been more palatable had it been a crime of passion.

Conflicted, I drew pictures with crayons and paper, encouraging Troy to draw as well. I drew what was real to me. Taking the sepia-brown crayon, I drew my mother's haunted eyes. He asked to borrow the crayon, and he drew what was real to him: a glass of Coca-Cola.

He grinned when I was asked for my autograph.

A guard passed us, saying to Troy, "Bierdz, button up your shirt."

Troy flinched, reminding me of a frightened Abu, and promptly grabbed at his shirt buttons. He looked down and noticed his top three were unbuttoned. He didn't know what to do with them. I watched him as he searched the room for a clue to the correct button regulations. Every other inmate in the room had only the top button unbuttoned. Fingers fumbling, he buttoned up his others.

His behavior was clearly fear-motivated, as if there could be repercussions. Sudden concern softened my hostility; I again asked him how he was treated. He said C.C.P. was good. He mentioned being transferred and pleaded with me to stop it. I talked gingerly about his having delusions, which he denied.

He said he liked it at C.C.P. He liked his "room." He watched his TV. He ate food. His life was okay.

Changing the subject, with intent to bring it up later, I asked him which of the postcards I sent him had he kept.

"I didn't keep any of them," he replied.

"Oh," I said, surprised, "that's okay. I just wondered which ones you liked best. Why don't you save them? Then you can look at them more than once."

"I didn't know I can save them."

"Yeah, I thought you knew that. You can keep up to fifty. Any more than that is a fire hazard."

His eyes teared. I asked him why.

"I cried in my cell about Mom again," he said finally.

"Oh?" I started gently, suspicious. "What about Mom?"

He looked down, focusing on a pencil.

There was no way I was going to drop this. "Was it because you won't get out for a long time?"

He was absolutely still.

"Did you cry because you miss Mom?" That's what I really wanted to know.

Troy shuffled his feet, but he gave me no response. "Or do you cry when I come into town? Because of me?"

Five minutes later, I still hadn't received an answer

"Do you want a Kit Kat?" I changed the subject.

He looked up and uncrossed his legs. He looked at the vending machines. His mood lifted, because of the promise of a candy bar.

A Kit Kat didn't make it all better, but Troy lived very much in the moment, so it helped. I watched him enjoy his candy. One hundred percent of him was enjoying it. There's freedom in being in the moment, and Troy found that freedom, perhaps the only freedom he'd ever know.

I watched him carefully unwrap the last bite of his Kit Kat, place it in his mouth, lean back in his chair, and close his eyes. In my hand was a crinkled wrapper of a candy bar I had eaten less than five minutes before. With all my faculties, I tried to remember the taste of it. I couldn't. What was it like to taste food the way he did? I wanted to feel the delight my brother felt. Smoothing out the crinkled wrapper, I wiped it against my tongue.

An incredible thing happened then.

I tasted chocolate for the first time. Contrary to popular belief, chocolate is not just smooth or creamy. Chocolate is scarlet. Chocolate is alive. Chocolate rhymes.

As I tilted my head back and closed my eyes, I shared my new feelings about chocolate aloud.

"Do you want to play?" I asked him.

"Chocolate's not alive," he said.

Digesting his response, I decided to change the subject to something more logical, to make him feel more comfortable. Before I said another word, he sighed, "Chocolate's like just being born."

He was lying back in his chair, eyes closed.

"Oh, is that right?" I smiled, charmed.

"Chocolate is an airplane," he said.

"Chocolate is an airplane, you're absolutely right," I said, warmly. Suddenly I could drop my judgment of him. His motives and actions with my mother didn't seem to matter any more.

He mimicked the noise of an airplane. He laughed, feeling silly. Putting my arms out like wings, I mimicked the sound of an airplane too. I never felt so free.

"We did this when we were kids," he said.

And his arms went up and he was an airplane too.

It was a beautiful moment – we were off to another world – two brothers – flying.

Both of us free.

Both of us strong.

Both of us unlimited.

But his joy soon passed. He looked upset, "I'm going to Hell."

I once again explained, "Mom forgives you."

"But the *Kenosha News* won't. I'm going to Hell."

"The only place you are going is another prison in Winnebago."

He was petrified. "Don't let them take me out of here."

"I don't want them to but what can I do about it?"

"I don't deserve Hell."

"You have to trust me. I don't think you can trust your own mind right now. You're not going to Hell."

"The *Kenosha News!*"

"If I get you the note – clearing you of your old route – you'll agree that you're not going to Hell?"

"Of course!"

"Okay, then, I'll do it. And then Mike will see you don't need to be transferred. We want to keep you right here."

"FANTASY ESCAPE"

41

Saving Troy At
The *Kenosha News*

December 27, 1994

On the way to the *Kenosha News*, I stopped to phone Hope, in order to explain why I needed to go there.

She agreed that she didn't want Troy transferred, so I should to go to the newspaper. But she feared I'd inadvertently give them a story they'd publish, and it would bring up everything from the past, and this time, not only she, but little Julia could be emotionally scarred.

I was about to walk a tightrope.

The *Kenosha News* offices were on three floors. Guessing that the Circulation Department on the lowest level would be able to help me, I started there.

As soon as I walked in, all six employees stared at me from their desks. I didn't expect to be on stage. It reminded me of my only high school theater audition, which petrified me to the point that I never auditioned for theater again. I forced a laugh, self-conscious, "Aah...I'm not sure...who I should speak to," I gulped.

A heavy brunette secured most of my attention.

"What do you need exactly?" she asked.

My mouth went dry. I could not speak. I could not emit a sound. There was too much pressure. Troy's future depended on the words I chose. Finally, I got out, "Aah...I...need to know the name of one of your carriers."

"Are you a customer?"

"Aah, no, I'm not."

"We can't release that information to the public."

She walked away.

I froze. This was much too important for me. But maybe if I could make myself be somebody else, I could free myself up enough to communicate. I tried to be one of my characters, like outgoing Jake, "Miss, if you could come back here a sec. It's personal."

Reluctantly, she moved to the counter.

Still trying to be Jake, I flashed her Troy's two-week notice, "Troy used to be a newspaper boy ten years ago."

Jake would not have broken eye-contact, but I did. I didn't have the concentration. I hated myself for being weak.

"Troy's a paranoid schizophrenic..." I stammered, "...and still thinks he has the route. He thinks he's going to Hell for not ever quitting the route. He thinks the papers haven't been delivered since. If you could give me the name of a new carrier, or write on a piece of *Kenosha News* stationery that you received his two-week notice, or that you forgive him, it would really help us out."

I was close to tears, but the woman was indifferent. "I don't think we can do that," she said, "but I guess I'll go check with my manager."

She went into a glass cubicle and talked to a man – for minutes – my request should've only taken seconds to communicate.

Finally, she returned saying, "We're not authorized to do that."

It felt like a truck had barreled into me. I whispered angrily, "He thinks he's going to Hell because he didn't quit his route."

"That's so sad," she said, walking away.

I marched to the next level. Advertising. I told myself I needed to be assertive like my personality Joey, the six-foot-five body-builder.

A woman with blond hair was taking advertising information over the phone and typing on her computer. She put her call on hold, smiled, and nodded.

Her smile cancelled my need to be Joey. I tried to figure out who I should be, while I said, "I just came from Circulation, and they refused to help my brother. Do you have a brother?"

I hated myself for sounding scattered and unfocused, but I didn't know who I was "being"

She shook her head "no" to answer my question, and raised her eyebrows at my emotion.

"My brother used to be a paperboy with you guys."

"We have over a hundred paperboys."

"Could you do me a favor?"

"What?"

"Would you just write a short note for me?"

"I'm supposed to be working."

"This'll only take a second."

"What should I write?"

I gave her Troy's note. As she read it, I said, "My little brother used to be a paperboy ten years ago. He thinks the newspapers haven't been delivered since. Can you believe that? He never quit. This is what he gave me – his two-week notice. I don't need the name of who took over his route. I don't need any names."

"I'm so sorry," she said.

"If you could just write 'I forgive you' on a piece of *Kenosha News* stationery."

Her forehead layered with wrinkles of sympathy. "Let me see if I'm authorized to do that."

"I give you the required authorization."

She smiled, "Mr. Brandt owns the paper."

I wanted to avoid Mr. Brandt. I had to avoid a newspaper story, for Hope's sake.

"This is really important, okay?" I said. "He thinks he's headed for Hell. I'm not requesting something really big, you know."

"Why don't you go up to the third floor and talk to Mr. Brandt."

I slowly walked up the last flight of stairs. Shuffling into the mahogany-lined room, I whispered to the ancient secretary, "I'm looking for Mr. Brandt."

"You came to the right place. You are?"

"Thom...ah...Zoey Drake."

"There he is," she said, indicating the 60-ish man rounding the paneled cubicles. "Why don't you have a seat over there," the secretary said.

I tried to relax in the large leather chair. I closed my eyes and tried to imagine myself as Joey again.

Mr. Brandt met my hand as I extended it into his pathway.

"Mr. Brandt, I'm...Zoey Drake."

He smiled, studying me.

"Actually," I said, losing Joey completely, and hating myself for my weak concentration, "I have just a little...ah...it's hardly anything at all. I don't know why it's become such a big deal." I was too upset to speak. No other words came out.

Mr. Brandt's open hand guided me into his office. His large antique desk dominated a third of the generous space. Outside his window was a three-story cobblestone building selling American dinnerware. His bulletin board was crowded with awards and historic photos.

"I went downstairs to Circulation, then to Advertising...all I want is a little favor...it's not even a favor, really. I just need a little piece of paper with some words on it." I grabbed a pen and pointed it at a pad of paper on his desk. "My bother is in prison for life. He can't hurt anybody. He's a paranoid schizophrenic."

He looked at me with concern. He read Troy's note.

"The name you gave me, 'Drake,' it confused me. You're one of the Bierdz's, aren't you?" He was calm. Each syllable he spoke was enunciated perfectly and he paused between sentences.

"Bierdz?" I said.

His secretary told him he had a phone call. He excused himself, taking it at his desk. I didn't pretend not to listen to his phone conversation. That's exactly what I was doing. Listening. And Mr. Brandt included me in with an occasional glance.

He spoke into the phone, then whispered to me, "I have the privilege to tell you good news. Within the last two months, I've had two grandsons. Now the good news: neither of them looks like me," he smiled.

After he hung up the phone, he asked what I did. I told him I had been an actor, but my acting days were over.

He said he knew my mother from years ago, when she pestered him about getting my picture in the paper after I'd done my first commercial.

"I'm sure I can help you with this," he said. "I know everything about your acting career."

"Ahuh," I muttered.

He rose, taking Troy's note.

Defiantly, I stood up, protective of the note, "I don't want you to do a story. I just want somebody to sign a piece of *Kenosha News* stationery."

"You can have this note back in a minute," he said, "I just have to take it down to the head of the legal department."

I didn't know what to do. I needed Mr. Brandt to help save Troy from his idea of Hell. I nodded my approval to Brandt, but locked eyes with him in warning.

He looked around the room, affable. "Let me see. I should find you a book to look at while I'm out of the room." He fingered a row of timeworn books, decided on the *Guinness Book Of Sports Records*, and handed it over.

Mr. Brandt went downstairs trying to figure out a way to milk the story, I assumed. Kenosha was a small town, I thought. Not much news happened there.

Brandt returned and caught me staring at a picture of an athlete in a Speedo. I closed the book nervously. "I'm not here to do a story," I reminded him, sternly.

"Yes, I know. But I'm a newspaper man," he continued with an explanation. "Why not a little publicity for yourself?"

"No."

"Why?"

"Who cares why? My sister. She's afraid of the publicity."

"I don't see what your sister has to do with anything."

"She doesn't want to be reminded of our mother's murder."

The room got quiet. He was pensive. We both were.

"But if you're a good actor and you continue to work, then she will be faced with publicity at some time."

"Not now, okay?"

"You're in the company of some very important actors," he coaxed, gazing at his bulletin board.

"I know."

"Al Molinaro is from Kenosha," he said. "He played Al on *Happy Days*."

"My Grampa met him once."

"Dan Travanti *of Hill Street Blues* is from Kenosha."

"My mother went to school with him."

"Don Ameche never felt much loyalty to Kenosha."

"Oh."

"Orson Welles."

"I don't care about acting anymore. I really don't. I don't like people watching me."

He weighed the next words in his head. He put Troy's note down. I slid it closer to me.

"That must have been a very difficult time for you and your family."

"Yes...but..."

There was a knock on the door. As I turned, a middle-aged man stepped in the doorway holding a camera. I was on guard.

The photographer said, "We have to get that picture of you with the wreath that lady made."

Friendly Mr. Brandt smiled his consent. I grew paranoid that they were trying to sneak a photo of me. Mr. Brandt asked me to follow him, so I could see the wreath a reader made from folded up newspapers. As soon as I caught a glimpse of it, I quickly dodged back into his office and waited for his return.

He came in, saying, "It's a shame to let a Kenosha actor leave the building without getting an interview. Since we have time, why not?"

"I'm not here to do a story."

"But you're a soap opera actor from Kenosha."

"I don't care about acting or anything, just get me the note forgiving Troy. Please."

He left the room and returned in ten minutes. I watched him as he picked up a pen and copied what his lawyer had typed.

> Dear Troy,
> Your brother, Thom Bierdz AKA Zoey Drake, asked that
> I write a letter to you relieving you of all responsibilities
> as regards to your previous newspaper route. Please be
> assured that your route has been reassigned and that
> we appreciate your service as a carrier.

He gave the note to me, then folded Troy's two-week notice and inched it toward his drawer.

"I need to have that back," I said.

It wasn't the voice of towering Joey – or Jake – it was my voice. A strong, determined voice.

"TRAFFIC"

42

Impossible To Kill

December 28, 1994

I saw Troy walking toward me. I smiled broadly, confident. I had the goods.

There were only two other occupied tables. The below-zero winds had kept the regular visitors homebound.

"I've got good news," I said. Then I informed him I'd located two of the four girlfriends. One was married with children. The other was engaged. I was able to prove to Troy that I talked to the engaged one, because on the phone she told me he'd sent her two letters last month. Troy had never mentioned the letters to me. He believed me when I told him, truthfully, that the girls forgave him, wished him the best, and accepted their break-ups.

I explained I could not locate the other girls. That meant they had changed their names by marrying, or they had moved out of Kenosha. Either way, they were obviously not still dating Troy.

He accepted my news with visible relief.

"The *Kenosha News*?" he asked, turning anxious again.

Proudly, I recapped the whole story, dancing gingerly around words that could upset him. Words like "my brother is a paranoid schizophrenic." But looking into his wide, chestnut eyes, I couldn't withhold everything from him. I admitted that I said at the *Kenosha News*, "my brother...*might* be a paranoid schizophrenic and he...*we* want to make sure his paper route is covered."

He broke. He burst into tears, then recoiled as quickly.

"I shouldn't have killed Mom," he cried. "It was a dumb thing to do. I can't believe I did that. I shouldn't have killed her."

This burst of emotion touched me to no end.

"It's okay, though," I said. "You made a mistake."

"It was so dumb."

"I know. It was dumb. Mom was a very good lady. But what's done is done."

"She's still angry at me. How could she not be?"

"She's not angry at you, Troy."

He paused for a long while, finally saying, "I was thinking...maybe... I hit her head so hard...because I thought it was full of rocks, like she always told me mine was."

I wasn't going to let him get away with that lame excuse.

"Troy, her head wasn't full of rocks, was it? You banged her head open. Did you see any rocks?"

As he shivered next to me, I could tell he was picturing the murder scene, splatters of her brain all across the room, but no rocks.

"Troy..." I relented, "she's okay now, though. She really is."

This seemed an appropriate opportunity to relate the message she'd sent through psychic Gary to get me to visit Troy in prison. He digested it, his eyes never leaving mine.

"You have to forgive yourself. Mom forgives you. If you make yourself a good life now, if you help people, you'll be happier."

"I found out something."

"What?"

"Zo, a person can't kill his mother."

I wasn't following him.

"I didn't do that. You felt her after she died and I did, too. I messed her up maybe, but I didn't kill her."

At long last, we were on the same wavelength. I was impressed he could see things from a spiritually evolved perspective.

"Nope. You didn't hurt her at all. Not really. Just the physical dimension, which really is nothing."

"I killed me, instead of her, by accident. But that's what happens when you try to kill someone. You kill yourself by accident."

He wrote:

> mircinary hopes and
> Dreams of a mircinary
> Are only hopes and
> Dreams of a mircinary
> no one can touch him
> no one can help him
> start his memory over
> and over again.
> troy

I suggested he write a letter to himself at five years of age. What would he tell himself then to prevent upcoming pain?

dear little five year old troy

look out for black outs or what ever its call when you feel you are uncontrollable for a second. I would hold you hand and hold my own hand because its hard in life when you feel that you cant cry. and when you would be happier crying and cant cry because your body doent let you when you think you could only be seeing black when you can see perfectly fine and calling it a black out when you kill your mother

As I read his letter, he looked sullen.

He said, "I think I miss Mom more than you do. I lived with her."

"I know you do." I rubbed his back.

He was sweating as he said, "What bothers me most about her beating me up through all eternity is not that she's beating me up. It's that I'm going to have to go to the bathroom at some point."

"I don't think–"

"That's gonna be pretty weird."

There was nothing I could say to diminish his obscure worry. As I re-read his letter, he said he didn't believe his paper route was being done.

This exasperated me.

"I just talked to the head of the paper. You don't believe me?"

"I believe you," he said, "I just don't think they know the right houses on the route."

"They know. It's being done. You have the letter. What more proof do you need?"

"You have to watch it being done to make sure it is being done. That only makes sense"

"You want me to watch the boy deliver papers?"

"Yeah. You have to watch him."

"You wouldn't believe me, would you?" I asked.

"No. I'd have to see it being done myself."

"Troy, Mike may transfer you to Winnebago, you know."

Troy's eyes weren't facing in my direction, but I could tell he was staring at something. I followed them to the object of his fascination: a cockroach that had crawled up the table leg and was feasting on his sandwich wrapper.

Ten years ago, in school classrooms he tore insects apart. He watched them wriggle as their legs were removed one by one. Expecting him to torture this cockroach, I cringed and studied him, as he studied the insect.

He inched his fingers closer to it, slowly, deliberately, so as not to alert it. I felt a pain in my heart, like a pinch – a pain of empathy for the bug.

His fingers, now a few inches from the doomed insect, craned down, lifting the wrapper off the table. The roach tried to escape.

Until this point, Troy had shown no emotion. An earnest smile emerged as he slowly lowered the wrapper to the floor, and tipped it so the bug had an easy descent to freedom. As the roach scuttled away, the

"BIRDS AND CHAINS"

smile shifted from my brother's face to mine. Inside, my sympathy for the cockroach became the most sincere inner salute, commending my brother, if only mentally, for his momentous shift.

I felt an awkward silence coming, so I spoke the first thought that came to my mind.

"Do you remember our birds?" I asked.

"Star," he remembered.

"We both had birds named Star. I had a parakeet when I was 17. You had a little budgie for a short while," I went on, "at Mom's when you were 17."

"You had yours first."

"Well, I'm eight years older than you. You remember what happened to mine?"

"It flew away when you were practicing with a golf club in Dad's front yard."

"That summer I was living with Dad. Mom and I weren't getting along. I needed my space, and she wouldn't give it to me."

Troy seemed surprised. He nodded and looked down.

I continued. "At Dad's apartment, I had bonded more with Star. I thought that he would stay on my shoulder if I went outside. But when I walked outside, he flew away. My...Star...flew away."

"Of course it did."

"And do you remember what happened to yours?" I asked.

"Mom killed mine."

"Aah, she didn't kill it."

"She vacuumed it."

"She didn't mean to. She was cleaning its cage. She didn't know how strong the vacuum was," I said. "Don't you think that's weird? That we both had a bird we named Star? Do you know what symbolic is?"

He seemed tired and reluctant to continue his end of the dialogue.

"I flew to California," I prodded.

"What are you trying to say? Mom vacuumed me up?"

237

"Mom sucked the life out of your wings, in a way, by participating in your co-dependence. You're not very free in here, are you?"

"Mom did it to me?"

"No. You did it to yourself. You and Mom had a real strong bond, lots of love. You didn't have to kill her, Troy. She loved you so much. But you can't undo that."

"I'm going to Hell."

"It's okay. Come on, it's okay. Don't you worry. I'm not going to let you go to Hell. Mike won't either."

He was tired. I couldn't get him to share any more. Reminding him that this was our last visit this trip, I suggested we play a game – or talk – or read. Nothing I said kept his attention. Like a petulant child, he reclined in his chair and pretended to sleep.

I explained to him that the reason we tire is rarely physical exhaustion; we tire when the brain has received so much new stimuli it goes on overload. The brain needs to shut down and use sleep time to file the new information.

I realized I was undermining my own argument by giving him more information. With much regret, I conceded to our farewell.

I stood up, and told him to stand up. I hugged him for minutes, avoiding the eyes of the guard who would have reminded me this was against the rules. I could feel my brother's heart beat. He smelled like old cigarettes. At first he resisted our embrace. Then he held on to me tightly.

I whispered, "We all make mistakes."

I was referring to myself. When Troy was about a year old, and I was nine, and he destroyed my Hot Wheels city in the basement, I, his big brother, beat him. When Troy was 19, and I was 27, he killed our mother, and once again shattered my world. But this time his big brother didn't beat him. His big brother would never make that mistake again. This time his big brother was helping him pick up the pieces. And if I could do it all over again, I would change so many things. I would have been a better big brother when I was nine. Maybe this is a crazy thought, but that might have been enough to save our mother's life.

<u>COLD CELL</u>
Sitting in my cold cell,
stairing at the walls.
no-one their to listen,
no-one hears my calls.
darkness fills my cell,
yet, brightness through the hall.
soon begins the screaming,
that horifies us all.
i wish i could go back,
change what i have done.
yet, theirs no-one to go to...
no place to run...
— TROY BIERDZ

"We all make mistakes." I said again. "You keep looking for punishment. Punishment you think you deserve, but you are already being punished. That's what prison is. This is your punishment. You don't deserve any more. Nobody's going to beat you up for eternity."

He looked relieved.

"I love you, okay?" he said.

I inhaled deeply, and though I smelled my brother's sweat and smoke, there was also clean air there. I listened as the air filled my body and I felt whole and alive.

"Okay," I said.

43

Humility

1995 to 1999

By 1995, I was running out of money, and needed a job. A past co-star on *Y&R*, who also needed money, called me about selling no-run pantyhose. She explained it was a network marketing operation. If we got people to sign up under us, we'd make a commission off their sales, plus a commission off the people they signed up, and so on. Nobody bought these pantyhose. It was amusing and humbling.

I was still looking for ways to make money in 1996, when a friend offered to sell my soap memorabilia on eBay. After she sold these, I wondered what else people might buy. Balancing on the thin line between being resourceful and being desperate, I sold my underwear. My worn jockeys got about sixty bucks a pair until new eBay restrictions stepped in the way. I didn't sell enough underwear to pay the rent, so I began working for another friend at Swing Café, a West Hollywood coffee shop.

I made cappuccinos for six dollars an hour. It had been over a decade since one of my customers at Your Place bar had tipped me a dollar a drink, warning me to not lose my humility. Making cappuccinos and hoping for a twenty-five cent tip was a humbling experience for me. Humility builds character, or so the saying suggests. But through this supposed character building, I felt shades of shame, resentment, anger, and bitterness.

Around West Hollywood grocery stores, I occasionally saw a very beautiful man. I pretty much stalked him for months, following him with my phone number until he eventually decided to call me. He was 31-year-old waiter, Doug Bisson, with no interest in a boyfriend at that time. I asked him out anyway, and was endeared to his very grounded attitude about life that was very different than mine. Like few people in Hollywood, Doug had absolutely no interest in the entertainment business, no hidden agenda, no drive to accomplish, and lived perfectly in the moment, happy as could be. He was as nice a guy as Big Dog, and also as loyal.

Doug helped me make peace with being a soap opera has-been working at a coffee shop. He helped me focus on what was really important: waking up each day with integrity, being healthy, and having fun.

In 1997, my dad was writing a novel and to do research he took me with him to Poland. It was a great vacation, except for his smoking in the car aggravating my asthma. We bonded as we examined thousand-year-old buildings and hoped someday to return to this magic place with our partners.

Back in L.A., I tired of groveling for coffee house tips, so I jumped at the chance when offered fifteen bucks an hour to bartend and/or be a waiter with a Hollywood catering company. On these nightly events, I was to dress in my thrift-shop tuxedo and show up at an address – sometimes a business, sometimes a private home. I bartended for many celebrities: Joan Collins, Rob Reiner, Tom Hanks, Don Rickles, Barbara Sinatra. And every A-list personality was at these parties. Even Doug was impressed.

These were exciting, if still humbling, experiences. But I had no idea I was to face the *most* humbling experience of my life in March 1999.

• • •

I was given no information other than to be at Raleigh Studios at 7:00 PM. I hadn't been to that studio since I filmed my first TV commercial for Dr. Pepper there fifteen years earlier.

I walked into the movie soundstage to find other caterers stocking bars and hanging streamers. Glitter was pumped into the air from an automated fan above the dance floor where huge mirror balls spun. I approached the catering captain.

She asked, "And you are?"

"TABLES TURNING"

"Zoey Drake. What is this? Looks "glamorous.""

"Nothing more glamorous than daytime TV."

"Daytime TV?"

"*Soap Opera Digest* Awards."

I panicked, remembering that about ten years earlier I was a presenter at these awards, giving the statue to winner Anne Heche.

The captain said, "Follow me to your bartending station." She led me to the main bar where caterers were busy stocking glasses and liquor.

"I'm not sure if I'm feeling okay," I said.

"We're overstaffed, so if you want to go, let me know in a few minutes."

"Thanks. I need to go to the bathroom a sec."

Catching my breath, I walked down studio streets to find the staff restroom. I wondered if I should get out of there quickly, before anybody I used to work with saw me. I couldn't face them, not after I blew off my farewell party, and left them waiting for me holding a cake. Besides doting Jeanne Cooper, and the soap alumni involved in marketing pantyhose, I'd never contacted any of the people I had worked with, "flubbed" scenes with, even shared dressing rooms with. I couldn't face the looks of sympathy, or pity, I would now receive from them. I'd believed I could run away and never face them again, like I had run away from almost everyone I knew in Kenosha and Milwaukee.

I adjusted my bowtie in the mirror, thinking what a horrible scenario this was. I couldn't believe it had happened. Still, with all my spiritual reading, I wondered if I hadn't on a very subconscious level willed this drama to take place.

I was shaking. My heart was pumping. After I used my inhaler, I wondered what would happen if I went back into the studio and bartended? Could I do that? Did I have the guts to look my fellow actors in the face? What would they think of me? What would I think of me? I became curious enough to walk back to the studio. It's not like I could be beaten-up or murdered. I would just turn about a hundred shades of red.

I debated whether or not to try to be one of my characters to get through this night. But they failed me at the *Kenosha News*, so I decided I needed a guaranteed way to relax – Tequila.

Heading back to the soundstage, I passed a vending machine. It had a Kit Kat. I remembered how Troy was able to connect so fully with that one thing – the chocolate. Nothing else mattered.

I bought a Kit Kat, then told the captain I felt better and was ready to bartend. I chugged Tequila, but not enough to appear drunk.

Soon the place was packed. I recognized dozens of daytime stars, and they recognized me too. Tricia Cast, my wife on *Y&R*, excitedly came to my bar to talk to me. Lauralee Bell came too.

Waiter friends of mine, who passed hors d'oeuvres that night, told me they heard I was bartending in order to work the pity angle and get publicity to get back on the show.

And I told this to the reporter who wanted to interview me, after I made him his drink. I also said maybe I deserved this for not showing up at my goodbye party.

He said, "Nobody deserves this. Not even Tonya Harding."

The truth was I needed the fifteen dollars an hour.

44

Another Bierdz Murder

August 1999

Surfing the net while Doug was asleep, I found a news article about another Bierdz murder. The perpetrator's name was Denny Bierdz. I later learned our grandfathers were cousins. Denny and his immediate family lived in a Chicago superb one hour from Kenosha.

I was able to contact Denny's brother. His name was Tom Bierdz. Tom and I were close in age, had the same name, had siblings murder a family member, and astonishingly, we both had mothers named Phyllis. We were both self-professed neurotic writers with similar intentions – his web address had the words peace and forgiveness in it. Heterosexual Tom was a doctor and better versed in science than I, and we had many significant conversations about family genetics. He did not feel Denny was a schizophrenic, but rather that he had paranoid tendencies.

As a child, Denny suffered from obsessive-compulsive disorder. Leaving his bedroom for school, he checked for up to forty-five minutes, to see if the doorknob was unlocked. His parents grew tired of his behavior and removed the doorknob altogether. That didn't solve his problem. His obsessive-compulsive disorder manifested in other ways.

In school Denny complained of bad vision. His parents took him to an eye doctor. The doctor said there was nothing wrong with his sight. Nevertheless, Denny believed his sight was steadily becoming blurry. His parents took him to a psychiatrist to find out why Denny was making up these lies. Denny refused to admit he was inventing the blindness, because in actuality he was not making it up. In several years, another doctor would finally discover Denny *did* have a very rare vision disorder. By that point, Denny had already distanced himself from most people. He realized not only was his sight deteriorating, but so was the reliability of medicine, and the reliability of family. This led Denny, even though he retained little vision, to be very self-reliant as an adult, and also extremely controlling of his surroundings.

He fell in love with Deborah. They had five kids.

It was not a good relationship. He was verbally and emotionally abusive to her. She divorced him. But he still wanted to be married to her. He believed he still had a right to her.

On August 15, 1999, Denny, 38, optimistically told his father he was going to see if Deborah would take him back. Denny went to the house where he used to live; where Deborah and their five children still lived.

Deborah did not want to get back together with him. He told her if he couldn't have her, then no one could. She called the police. He ripped off her clothes trying to rape her. She escaped to the driveway. He tackled her there and stabbed her with a kitchen knife.

Two of the kids watched in horror as their father kept stabbing their mother. Police showed up and pointed their guns at Denny, ordering him to stop stabbing his wife. He would not. The police fired bullets at Denny until he was dead.

That night, Denny and Deborah Bierdz were both killed in front of their children.

This was horribly devastating to me, because I understood how much the children would always hurt. When I shared this with Doug, he absorbed the information less personally, like he was reading a tragic book. He didn't understand. He'd never met my mom, or Troy, and though he knew Hope and Gregg, they did not show their pain. Neither did my father.

I had never asked Doug if he were concerned to be in a relationship with me, since my family had mental illness. But when my father visited along with his extremely likable and intelligent wife, Sue, they asked

Doug if he had any worries being with me. Doug said no. Dad asked if Doug worried that in the future I might go crazy. What Dad didn't understand about Doug, and why I felt so comfortable with Doug, was that he never thought about the future at all. He amazingly enjoyed life in the present all the time.

Something I have never done.

45

Paranoia

T he only constant in Gregg and Patsy's eight years as an on-again, off-again couple was their relationship getting worse. Married for five years, they had two small children and a live-in nanny. These daily "witnesses" didn't do much to ease the tension. Patsy was still insecure, jealous, and high-maintenance. Gregg was now resentful, uncommunicative, unsure he wanted to be married, and, having quit the agency when he wasn't promoted, unemployed.

After failing as an actor and an agent, Gregg tried screenwriting. He said his script was about seduction, comparing it to the movie *Gods And Monsters*. I never saw this screenplay, and to my knowledge Gregg never finished it, instead he decided to become a literary manager. Unwilling to work his way up through an established company, he started his own small firm with Patsy's financial support. He proudly showed me his tiny office in a rundown building in Hollywood. He loved that little space more than the million-dollar mansion where he lived. It gave him breathing room. It empowered him – as much as his own "space" paid for with his wife's money could.

Patsy naturally expected a return on her investment. She had done everything she could to please her man; a man she loved deeply, and empowered, giving him a monthly distribution of money, a "nest-egg" of twenty-seven-thousand dollars, a car, fancy gym membership, and fashionable clothes. She even had cosmetic surgery. All she wanted was her husband's love and physical affection.

That October, the police were called to their house for the couple's worst fight. Gregg accused Patsy of physically assaulting him, and twisting his genitals, because he was not performing his husbandly duties.

After this incident, Gregg moved out, or was thrown out, of their house for good. Besides the "genital assault," Gregg added another new "twist" to this separation. He told me, our entire family, and all his friends that he was afraid Patsy was planning to kill him. I dismissed his fear as irrational. Dad did as well, saying that when he and Mom separated, Mom made similar threats.

As Gregg and Patsy's relationship was collapsing under the weight of their unrealistic expectations, my and Doug's relationship was going well. But truth be told, we'd been together for several years by then, and the romance was naturally decreasing. However, the bond Doug and I shared was as strong as most heterosexual married couples, and we subconsciously felt ready for a shift from honeymooners to parents. Incorrectly believing I'd overcome my allergies, I brought home to Doug our first "child," a German Shepherd pup called Bodhi. Naming the dog after the new-age bookstore, The Bodhi Tree, was my idea. Doug was not interested in The Bodhi Tree, but ironically, by being so connected to the present, he was the most spiritual person I knew.

Bodhi was my first pet since Abu, and my patience was being tested daily, especially now that I needed my inhaler again. But I never hit my beautiful little puppy, who was so sensitive and smart that he knew, without us punishing him, when he had done something "wrong."

I didn't want to raise the stress level in our little apartment by having Gregg stay with us, as he asked to, after leaving Patsy. Knowing what a discourteous roommate my brother had been in the past, I said he could only stay for a few days. I was relieved when Gregg left sooner than expected.

Fearing he wasn't safe enough from Patsy at my apartment, Gregg flew to Wisconsin and spent ten days with Hope. By November, he was back in L.A. and came over to my place with presents for his kids. He asked me to give them to his children for Christmas. I told him to do it himself; that Patsy, who had calmed down, would certainly let him see his kids during the holidays. Gregg begged me to hold onto the gifts. He also asked me to look in on the kids if he or Patsy faced a tragic death or imprisonment. Once again, I thought he was being irrational to believe the threats Patsy yelled in her temper tantrums.

If they got divorced, Gregg believed that Patsy, as the woman – a very rich woman – would be awarded custody of their children. I could not deny that he was probably right. He said he loved his kids so much that it would be unbearable to be without them. I tried to reassure him by reminding him Dad got visitation every other week after our parents split up.

Although Gregg never said anything when we were children, he blamed our father for our parents' divorce. Gregg was afraid his kids would blame him for his and Patsy's divorce, and make fun of him like we did our own father. He also said Patsy threatened to deny him any visitation if he proceeded with the divorce.

He didn't know what to do. He was terrified in his wife's presence, but he craved his children's companionship. His kids were the only thing in life he had left to hold on to; the only thing that gave him any sense of worth, pride, security, substance, importance.

I could not understand needing a child the way he needed his children. He needed his kids as much as he needed to breathe. As much as our mother needed us. He said he would die for them. Which made no sense to me. He said he would die for them if it made their lives easier.

I remembered our Mom saying something similar.

There was something beautiful, but also unsettling, in that sentiment. Suddenly, it hit me. What the missing piece of the puzzle might be. What really might have happened the night of July 14, 1989.

46

Mom's Secret

November 1999

As Gregg drove away, I raced Bodhi up and down the street. I thought about what it was like to be a parent. I would do anything for Bodhi. I could only imagine the love Gregg felt for his kids, and the love Mom felt for us.

If our mother had one wish, it was to guarantee her four children safety and happiness. She was the child of a secure two-parent home. When our father stunned her by bailing out of their marriage, her primary concern became her children's well being. She pledged to work overtime to create a secure and stable family for us. When we were kids, she made us promise we would always be together, even in adulthood, the five of us, safe and happy together. And if something ever happened to her, like a heart attack at age 92, we had to promise that the four of us kids would always remain close, always be there for each other in her absence. For the most part since her death, none of us had lived up to that promise.

She also wanted to take care of us financially, and chose a life insurance company that tripled our small inheritances in the event of her murder. Many life insurance policies have this clause, but her original one did not. We later found out that a short time before her murder, she changed her insurance policy.

Did she know she would die? Did she want to die? In other words, was she willing to be the one that had to die at Troy's hands?

The memory of her hugging me in her driveway the last time I saw her, not long before her death, replayed again in slow motion. My mother was sobbing. I had thought I read her mind, and was consoling her with, "Don't worry about me. I'm not going to die in a car accident on the way back to California." Then I added, "You're going to see me again!"

She knew she would not.

She knew she would die soon. Did she know because she was in on it?

Help would not come. The doctors and hospitals and courts were waiting for a corpse. She had a son who was so sick he existed to hear bones crack, and she had three other children's bones to protect from him. She knew if Troy killed, he'd be put in an institution for good. At last, he might get the care he needed.

I phoned Hope.

She said, "The last time I saw Mom and I asked her if she was going to be okay, she said yes. But I also wonder if she was ready to die. She seemed to be more at peace and not bothered by anything he did, or threatened, anymore."

There was nothing Mom could do to get the courts or halfway houses to help Troy. As it was, he was supposed to be serving a sentence at the frighteningly lax Exlogry House. She saw and understood the danger of it. She had to figure out a way to get him institutionalized before he would kill someone.

"She wouldn't have egged him on to kill her, but she would have stood there and taken it, I think," Hope agreed.

"There was no way she was going to let Troy kill one of us."

"I know," she said, confused. "She promised me that she'd never let Troy hurt me."

"She said that? Those words?"

"And to Gregg too. A week before she died. He said Mom promised him that Troy would never hurt him."

"You think that's what she was calling me about? I never returned her last phone calls to me."

"I shouldn't have left her. I asked her if she'd be alright and she said yes."

"Hope, Mom didn't have to invite him home like she did. She did it the minute she heard he was sentenced back to that lame excuse for a halfway house. And she had a chance to run out after you left. She had a chance to fight him with the bat, too. There were four blows, and no indication that she fought back, if you ask me. She sat in the car, within earshot as he asked for a gun to kill her with."

"He was talking all the time about killing you, Tommy, or Zoey. And all of us in a blaze of glory."

"She knew he would make good on his threats. She saw it escalating."

"I know," she said.

"She saw him getting more and more violent. She knew he was going to kill a human being soon. She saw his secret list of items needed to kill. She was in on it."

"To save us?"

"Troy said she 'asked for it.' Do you think she actually–"

"No way do I believe that."

"How did she know they'd get him before he got to California?"

"Aunt Mary told me Mom had been telling her that all four of us kids were adults and her work was done. She said Mom was tired and ready to go on. Mom also asked her a short while before that night, how long a drive it was from Wisconsin to California. Aunt Mary told her two or three days. She used to do it when she was in her 20s."

I told Hope, "If Troy drove to California, then by the time he got to me, I would have been warned. Was she calling to say she was sacrificing her life for me?"

"I don't know," Hope said. "She probably just wanted to hear your voice."

47

Gregg Won't Answer

January to May 2000

G regg moved back in with Patsy, and they were temporarily living in separate bedrooms. He didn't dare call me in December or January, because he knew if he told me about their possible reconciliation that I'd lecture him on how disastrous they were as a couple. If Patsy had threatened to kill him, as Gregg claimed, then why get back together with her? Troy threatened to kill Mom, yet she got back together with him, and he *did* kill her. I wanted no part of another potentially deadly relationship.

In February, Gregg finally phoned and said he and Patsy were officially splitting up. He asked me to help him move into a secured apartment building in the San Fernando Valley. I was thrilled that he was getting his own place, but only agreed to help if I didn't have to face any of Patsy's drama while we moved his things out of her house. Gregg assured me she would not be home.

But she was home, and, as I anticipated, she was overly emotional and weepy. I was furious at him for lying to manipulate me into doing what he wanted. The moment Gregg and I got back into his truck, I told him to drop me off at my apartment. I refused to help him move any further. It was raining and his mattress was in an open-bed truck. He sadly looked at me and asked, "How am I going to get this into my apartment by myself?"

I didn't care.

We had no reason to talk in March, April or May. Hope and Aunt

Mary were used to hearing from Gregg every week, but he also stopped calling them. Patsy called and told us he had gotten a minimum-wage book-stocking position at Brentano's bookstore in the Beverly Center Mall. Apparently Gregg was still living in his apartment, and saw his kids three times a week for the allotted two hours. Afterwards, he'd sometimes stay for the elegant candle-lit dinners Patsy prepared. She'd gotten a new hairstyle and some more minor cosmetic surgery. She was going to therapy for her anger issues, and her compulsion to once again keep Gregg on a "tight leash" by trying to buy him back. She liked tight leashes. Her dog wore an electronic collar that zapped him when he barked.

Ever since I lost my patience on Abu, I was extra sensitive to animals' feelings, therefore Bodhi, a barker, never wore a zapping collar. He rarely even wore a collar. Neither did the Chihuahua, Deen, that I'd bought Doug for Valentine's Day. Doug's smile stretched across his entire face when he saw the tiny puppy. That expression of delight on my partner's face was one I remembered well, as I used to have a similar effect on him when we first dated. In any respect, unlike Patsy's dog, our dogs were "children" in our "family." They ate anything we ate, often times getting portions equal to ours of whatever we cooked that was on sale at Ralph's grocery store. Because of my guilt over abusing Abu, I no longer ate meat, but Doug, Bodhi, and Deen did.

After dinner, Doug watched TV or fiddled with his cameras, as he had started to take pictures of the dogs. I lost myself painting for hours at a time. With Deen sitting in my lap, dripping paint onto our easy to clean wood floors didn't concern me, but I guiltily remembered all the paint I spilt on Big Dog's carpeting. Big Dog and I would still joke about it, and I was relieved when I learned his new boyfriend was a hairdresser, not a painter.

I thought about Rod, and wondered what his current relationship was like.

I thought about Gregg and Patsy, and didn't want to know any more about their current relationship.

But Hope was not as detached as I could be. She begged me to go knock on Gregg's door and plead with him to return her calls. I phoned Gregg and, getting his answering machine, left a stern message, then I drove to his place.

It was a security building and I was refused entrance. The guard called Gregg's apartment, but Gregg didn't answer. The guard left a message saying I was at the front gate. I waited a few minutes for Gregg to respond, then left.

The next night, Patsy called me, frantic. Gregg hadn't shown up for his scheduled Tuesday evening visitation with the kids. She wanted me to go to his building. I told her I wouldn't, because Doug and I were riveted to the latest TV phenomenon, *Who Wants To Be A Millionaire*? I told Patsy I'd tried to see Gregg the previous night and was denied entry. Nevertheless, she begged, and I finally relented.

Again, I was refused entrance. I told the guard I was Gregg's brother and needed to see him, because Gregg had been reclusive too long, and we were beginning to worry. He asked for my I.D. I showed him my driver's license, which read Zoey Drake, not Thom Bierdz. He asked why we had different names if we were brothers. I explained that Gregg had asked me to change my name. This only made the guard more suspicious of me.

I insisted we call the manager on premises. A petite woman came out in her robe. I told her that Gregg's wife and sister were concerned for his safety, and had asked me to check on him. The security guard phoned Gregg, but the phone line was busy. The manager guided me through the maze of brightly lit corridors and pointed to Gregg's door. We heard a continuous mechanical beep, similar to a phone off the hook. I knocked. If Gregg was in there, how could he put up with that annoying noise? Either he was not there, or he was unconscious inside the apartment.

"Gregg! It's me! Hope is mad at you!"

I kicked the door, but got no response.

The manager refused to use her key to enter, and said the authorities would have to intercede from this point.

The police arrived a half-hour later. They made me wait at the end of the hall while they broke down Gregg's door. It was chain-locked from the interior. The police kicked it open and disappeared inside. They must've hung up his phone because the beeping stopped. I froze, straining to hear some clue. I heard a few footsteps, then whispering, followed by a radio dispatcher.

I knew my brother was dead.

48

Gregg's Gone

May 22, 2000

The cops avoided my eyes when they came back into the hallway. One cop went downstairs, and I asked the other why. He whispered to me, staring straight into my eyes, that Gregg had shot himself. They had called the coroner, and the other cop would lead them up to the body.

It was unbelievable. Surreal. How could my sunny, charismatic brother kill himself? I asked the cop if he were sure it wasn't murder because Gregg and his wife had threatened each other. The cop told me the window in Gregg's apartment was locked from the inside. And with the door chain-locked, there was no way someone could have killed him and escaped.

I asked to see the body. The cop said it was against the rules. I said I needed to see it – that I had to see if he were really there or if this was some conspiracy. The cop told me not to tell anybody, but he would let me see the body as long as I didn't touch anything.

Gregg's apartment was beyond depressing – no furniture or lamps. The mattress had a blanket, but no sheets. Every inch of my apartment was covered in bright paintings; Gregg's walls were bare. I felt selfish for not bringing him art. There were no pictures at all, except for two framed photos of his children on the TV. A phone and an answering machine were on the floor. The police would discover many taped messages of Patsy screaming at Gregg. The message, from the night before, asking him to let me in, had been erased – so he must have been alive the preceding night.

Gregg's favorite books were in a paper bag. A few open cans of food sat on shuffled legal papers on the counter.

The old newspaper articles of Mom's murder jutted out of an envelope on the floor. He had highlighted facts and scribbled notes on these articles, like prospective titles, and later I would learn he was writing his own screenplay about Mom's murder.

I didn't understand how he could have made such a complete reversal on allowing our personal information into a screenplay; perhaps this showed just how desperate and out-of-character he had become in his final year. This new bit of insight into his last-ditch effort to either "cash in" on our family history or write a poignant motion picture, would lead me to forever question why he did not tell me. He had certainly known I'd wanted to work with him in the past, in any part of the entertainment industry. He also knew I had been writing Mom's story for at least a decade and I had offered, when I began writing, to split any profit with him and Hope. But Gregg took strides to keep the existence of his screenplay a secret from me – as if I needed any more reasons to be paranoid.

Aunt Mary later revealed to me that Patsy pushed Gregg to work harder on the screenplay and complete it, but apparently the subject matter devastated Gregg and each time he focused on it he sank into despair. Gregg did not have the spiritual beliefs that I did, which enabled me to "relive" the events of our family from a broader perspective and with some detachment.

Although I was affected each time I returned to these episodes, I did not share Gregg's belief that our lives were "fated," and therefore unalterable. I did not believe we were "doomed" to travel the road chosen for us.

I hated that I seemed to know less, not more, about Gregg, as we became men. I hated that we never worked well, or played well, together. I hated that I did not help him more, and did not have any indication he was suicidal. I hated that his apartment showed how severely depressed he was, and I hadn't known it.

His suicide note was addressed to Hope. He did not explain why he was killing himself, only that he wished for Hope to check in with his kids, and explain how much their daddy loved them.

There was a small hall leading to a closet and a bathroom. Gregg was in the closet – probably to muffle the noise – wearing jogging clothes and a robe, sitting with his legs spread. He was bloated, I was told, from having been dead for about twenty hours. A gun had fallen between his legs. His hands were not far from the gun. There was a little blood in the corner of his mouth, but I didn't see any other sign of injury. He was leaning back, his head between his Armani suits.

49

Losing My Mind

Summary 2000

Was Gregg's suicide a result of paranoia? Were his earlier attempts to conceal potentially damaging information about himself and our family also a form of paranoia? Was his refusal to share his personal life also a result of paranoia?

Were both my brothers paranoid?

Was I?

For many years in the 1990s, I worked on making a movie about my mother's murder, using dolls to play the characters. I resorted to this low-budget technique because I couldn't get my screenplay of her life to anybody in the industry. I *had* to get her story filmed somehow, to get it out of my head. This behavior might not be paranoid, but some might consider it obsessive or at least borderline crazy. To most of the entertainment industry, a doll movie depicting a family tragedy was more of an insane idea than an artistic one.

And what about the name change? There was nothing crazy about doing it to appease my family, but selecting the name "Zoey," as directed by a voice in a dream, as freakishly bizarre to people who hadn't spent a decade, as I had, trying to crack open my subconscious for guidance. And I thought I was starting to receive it. In the quiet before sleep, I was seeing faces and hearing voices. I was very proud, believing these visions and sounds were psychic progressions.

Was I psychic or psycho?

What if I weren't channeling other realms of consciousness at all?

What if I was beginning to hallucinate at random, as Troy, and maybe Gregg, had? Was I about to go crazy? Or was I already crazy?

Were all three Bierdz brothers crazy?

During these months I hardly left my apartment. Doug and our dogs brought me great comfort – especially Deen, the exact size of Abu, who would sleep in the small of my back. But they could do nothing to stop the terrifying scenes taking shape on my canvases.

The nights when Doug was away working, were the nights I understood for the first time why someone would kill himself. It was as if God no longer existed, or worse, that He stopped caring.

A feeling of utter desolation swept over me. I imagined it was what Gregg felt during his last weeks, and what Troy went through on a regular basis. It was as if nothing mattered. As if there was nothing but darkness and cold, with no promise of warmth, no promise of light. It was as if there were no life, just coldness, a constant coldness, and for that reason I needed to constantly pet my dogs, hold their paws. On the few occasions when Doug or the dogs weren't around, the heaviness of this desolation hit me so quickly it took great effort for me to move at all, even to a mirror to see who I was, what I was. In the darkness of night, I would force my tired, cold body out of bed and down the hall to the bathroom sink. I felt hollow. Catching a flicker of light from my neighbor's windows filled me with gratitude. It was as if I had been the only living being for centuries, and I had finally found another soul. All sounds became welcome miracles to my ears. I received a glimmer of hope there was life – outside – and, therefore, there might be life inside me too.

If this lack was my core belief, if this was my truest self, I did not want to acknowledge it. It was a sensation of such pessimism and despair I could easily become convinced that any attempt to outwit it was futile. Where did this dire blankness come from? Was it genetic? Was it Italian? Polish? Homosexual? Catholic? Mid-Western? Los Angelean? I didn't know. I only knew that it changed who I was.

The first moment I engaged with another human being after this desolate loneliness, I was so filled with gratitude I held back tears. I was suddenly changed from who I was and what I believed was real.

I wondered if many hermits suffered like this. I sometimes saw the hollow eyes of strangers, and wondered if they finally gave up trying to retrieve lives that were ripped away.

This depression was not mine; it was Gregg's. Suicide was contagious. Some of Gregg's friends experienced their deepest depressions at the same time.

Gregg might have benefited from medication. Troy certainly did; the year he was moved to the Winnebago facility, they perfectly balanced his anti-psychotic drugs and his delusions cut back so he could return, happily, to C.C.P. But medication was not my chosen cure for depression, nor my anxiety, which was certainly aggravated by using another type of drug, my inhaler, six times a day.

I became obsessed with exploring how my thought-patterns affected and created my lows, and my highs. Being a super-sensitive person must have had something to do with my moods, and my grandiose thoughts of wanting to help the world, to contribute in some way, and other over-achiever expectations must weigh down my brain – as well as set me up for extreme disappointment.

• • •

In my restless nights, I have asked my mother if she would come to me and show me what her life was like after death. And she never has. I have asked Gregg to come to me. He has appeared to me in dreams and talked to me, but I could not understand him. He projected happiness.

I didn't know if these were only dreams, or if they were visits. But I continually asked to know more, to see more, to feel more – more of what happened "out there." When I was a child condemned by the church, I asked for a God who loved me, and I received one. When I was a skinny gay bartender, I asked for a bigger world, and I became a soap opera star in Hollywood. When I asked for my dead mother to let me know if there was something that I, her selfish son, could do for her, she sent me an answer through Gary.

When the police told me that Gregg had killed himself, I asked to see him. Kneeling next to his dead body, crowded between his Armani suits, I recognized my hate and anger dissipating. I was no longer mad at him, because I saw he was not dead – only his body was. But it was so apparent his body had been vacated. It was only a shell. His chemistry and spirit, for which I was so in awe of him, were not in that body. Everything I knew him to be – the Gregg I loved, the Gregg I was jealous of, the Gregg who made me laugh – was not dead. Those Greggs weren't even in that closet.

What a gift it was to see his de-spirited body. I refused to see my mother's body after the murder because I thought I would actually believe she was dead. But while seeing Gregg's shell, I realized that seeing my mother's carcass would only have reaffirmed my suspicions that she was, indeed, alive – and definitely somewhere outside her body.

50

The Portrait

I brought a four-foot-tall package with me on my next trip to Kenosha. It was the wrapped portrait of my mother I had been painting.
My two little nieces, Julia and Jennifer, shifted their attention
from the baby dolls they were rocking and bottle-feeding to Hope as she
unwrapped the mysterious present. I sat next to her on the couch, beaming
with pride as she revealed the enormous acrylic face of my mother.

Julia asked, "Who is it?"

Hope tried to come up with an answer, but couldn't.

"That's Mom, Hope," I explained. "That was your grandma, girls.
She was a real special lady."

Hope coughed, and then said, "It is so...big. I mean...it's real nice of
you, but...I don't know, Tommy – Zo."

"I've been working on it for so long," my voice cracked. "I'll do you
one of Gregg, too."

"I don't think so."

She hugged me, and then rewrapped the picture with Julia's help.

Hope felt she should say something, "It's just so big. That's your
style. Not mine."

I couldn't believe she wouldn't give it a chance. "You could see it
even in the dark. I thought it might stop your nightmares."

Jennifer took the doll she was rocking and gave it to her mother to
make her feel better. She kissed Jennifer and gave the doll back. Hope
didn't look at me as she said, "And we never talked about that art film you

made about Mom and Troy. Doug said you entered your movie in a film festival and it won dolls or something? What was he talking about?"

"It didn't win dolls. I made the film with dolls and it won Best Experimental Feature in two of the three film festivals I entered so far."

"What did you do with dolls?"

"I did Mom's story. A few years ago. I knew it would make you upset, so I made Wisconsin into Idaho and changed everyone's names."

"With dolls?"

"And puppets. Over a hundred of them. I painted their faces with each bit of dialogue and I painted the sets. I had to tell her story, Hope, and I had no money to make a real movie or hire actors. So I got a camera and made a movie. Over an hour. A thousand cuts. Pretty complicated. I thought I'd lose my mind."

She raised her brows.

"I even burned myself," I rolled up my sleeve to show her my scarred bicep. "With the Troy doll's face in close-up, I cut to my own arm, which is supposed to look like the doll's arm, and I burned it with a cigarette like he did to test his pain threshold. I thought it would heal."

Her face was impossible to read.

"And since we're clearing the air, I'm going back to using my real name," I said, "Bierdz. Thom Bierdz. There's a sweet porcelain doll that's you."

Her face grew strained. "You showed this to strangers?"

"I changed my name for Gregg and for what? Go ahead and kill yourself if it's too painful to let me be who I really am."

"Zoey!"

"Thom. What? You have to do what your heart pulls you to do. Look at Gregg. He certainly wasn't honoring his true path. Who knows what he was thinking or feeling. You want me to keep all my frustrations inside myself like you and Gregg? I can't keep doing that. I have to let them out."

I headed out and drove my car to see Troy.

• • •

Troy met me at a table in the center of the visiting room. He wanted coffee and popcorn.

As he ate, I was curious about his reaction to Gregg's death. He hadn't mentioned it, not once over the phone, since I'd seen him months ago when I was in Wisconsin for the funeral.

"I still can't believe what Gregg did," I said.

"How come he did it?" he asked, very conversationally.

"His life was out of control, I guess, or not how he wanted it. A lot of people kill themselves. They get depressed and can't think straight. What an idiot to leave your kids behind like that."

"I can't believe he shot himself with a gun."

"Yeah."

"What kind of gun?"

"I don't know anything about guns."

"Gregg probably didn't either."

"Have you heard voices lately?"

"Nothing about Gregg."

"I think you ultimately have power over any voices," I said, then waited for him to follow my thought, "...but the voices are a scapegoat. You know you didn't have to kill Mom."

"I had to kill her."

"I don't think so. Do you really think so?"

"I don't know."

"Even if Mom didn't allow you to kill her, she would still have been accountable on a subconscious level. I have to believe that. I really have to. Because if not, then what is it all about? A totally random universe with no God watching over it? I can't believe that. I can't. I'd want to be dead. No, I wouldn't. I'd want to stop working so hard and trying so hard to get it right if no one cared and there wasn't a God."

"There is a God. The Bible says it."

"I cannot believe our fate is outside of ourselves, that we are victims and powerless. Look at Gregg, how he looked for power outside of himself, and then he was totally powerless with Patsy. But he didn't have to kill himself. He didn't have to be so damn depressed and haunted by it either. But he wanted things different. That's why people kill themselves. Because they can't accept life on anybody else's terms but their own. He wanted to see his kids all the time. Nothing wrong with that. But he couldn't, so he just should have moved away or something. Maybe to Europe. I'd rather be in another country than dead, you know?"

"Me, too."

"He got attached, too attached, to the idea that he had to see his kids everyday. And he got attached to a stupid view of who he was, like he was worthless, when he could've done anything, huh?"

"He was going to be a big agent."

"But before that. He had so many talents."

"He played basketball in high school."

"He was too short to play professionally. Patsy got what she was afraid of too. She was so afraid to be by herself that she had to have Gregg there, and she was way too controlling of him."

"Reminds me when Dad said Mom controlled him."

"Maybe. So Patsy, needing to be loved and needing to have someone be there for her until she died, wound up with a man who would rather be dead than with her. And she's a real looker, too. And Gregg feared he was weak and powerless and needed a wife who would convince him he was powerful, but the exact opposite happens when someone's needy like her. So needy."

"God must be punishing us."

"What do you mean?"

"Look what he does. You being gay. Me in prison."

"We're not victims of...tragedies."

"We're not?"

"We are more creators of tragedies."

"I don't know about that."

"Think about it. I'm so fucking needy sometimes. I needed to be famous and needed to look as good as I could, even having liposuction and my ears pinned back to look better, like those other soap opera studs.

I needed approval, then I needed to suffer for feeling guilty about my mother's death, and I created all kinds of hardships. I needed to be more famous than you and Gregg, needed to be the shining brother because I felt worthless and gay, but I thought I needed to hide the fact I was gay. I needed to tell Mom's story because I couldn't sleep, and I couldn't sleep because I needed to understand things that were out of my hands, and I needed to vent, but I still can't sleep. I lie awake wondering who I really am."

"You're Zoey Drake."

"I'm Thom Bierdz."

"You're Thom again?"

"Why not?" I smiled. "But I reserve the right to change it again if I want."

Troy and I sat back in our chairs. Through the far window I could see some inmates exercise in the courtyard.

"I got a new job," I said, "I needed money and I needed to get out of the apartment more so I could breathe."

"You got a job in a movie?"

"I got a job in a deli named Canters."

"You a cook again?"

"I'm a waiter again. At night, like ten at night to six in the morning."

"Who goes to eat at that time?"

"Night-owls and insomniacs. Kids from Goth clubs."

"The vampire types?"

"Yeah. They dress like vampires a little. We get some people in rock bands and other celebrities. I saw Darryl Hannah and Leonardo DiCaprio and Roseanne Barr. I've even waited on the new stars of *The Young and the Restless*, but they have no idea I used to be on it."

"Lauralee Bell who played Cricket?"

"No, but I was at a party once bartending for her parents, the *Y&R* producers. So embarrassing. As I handed them white wine, they told Jack Lemmon that years ago I used to be one of their actors."

"Ouch."

"I can't sleep, so why not wait tables? A lot of insomniacs eat Matzo ball soup. Some homeless people try to sleep in the booths."

"Do they let them?"

"No. But Canters has been around fifty years, and in the old days they used to give food to the needy. That's kind of cool."

He surprised me with, "Does Deen know you tried to drown Abu?"

"My Chihuahua?"

"Does he know?"

"I told little Deen, yeah," I said, red-faced. "But we get along good. Deen really loves me. He lies on his back in my arms, his legs in the air, and he sleeps on me like that."

• • •

My cheeks stayed flush with embarrassment the entire drive to Kenosha. I was the color of the aging crimson barns on the country roads a mile from my sister's house. Barns which existed before condominiums – before fast-food chains – before colleges – before automobiles – before my great-grandparents settled in Kenosha – certainly before my parents met as teenagers.

My blushed face was not the only thing exuding color that windy autumn day.

Everywhere I looked trees' leaves were turning hues – all the colors of the universe were represented – all sixty-four magnificent colors that I remembered from my deluxe box of Crayola crayons.

My red cheeks, or scarlet cheeks, or crimson, pink, maroon cheeks would exist until I could forgive myself for my actions against helpless Abu.

I didn't know it at the time, but each trip to Kenosha had been a journey of forgiveness.

Forgiving Dad for leaving Mom.

Forgiving Mom for being controlling and over-protective.

Forgiving Gregg for "having it all."
Forgiving Hope for being so conventional.
Forgiving Troy for the murder of our beloved mother.
Forgiving myself for hurting Abu.
And forgiving myself for being shy and scared and gay and weak.

51

Forgiving Troy

Hope didn't explain her change of heart when she joined me on the long drive to C.C.P. We listened to love songs and marveled at the trees changing colors. She looked different to me now – older – prettier. I'd never noticed what a commercially beautiful smile she had. Her teeth were as straight and white as mine, and she didn't even have veneers.

She was my one and only sister and I loved her deeply, which was easy to do considering she had the qualities I most admired from Mom – honesty, integrity, and endless devotion to her children. Hope was also a "survivor." We were both survivors. We just had different ways of doing it.

When she asked about the visiting area where she would see Troy, her smile fell and her eyes glazed and both of her hands gripped the steering wheel, inadvertently trapping some of her sweatshirt. Once inside the parking lot, she became emotionless. The tall barbed wire fences and lookout towers did not seem to comfort her.

Like an old pro, I showed her how to sign her admittance form for the guard and present her ID. We put our wallets and keys in one locker, put ten dollars in quarters in a baggie, checked our shoes with the guard, went through security clearance, had our hands stamped, and then we shuffled through the double electric doors toward the black-lit security checkpoint.

Stepping into the visiting area, she did not show her anxiety and instead tried to smile as she politely greeted the friendly officer in charge, who pointed us to our assigned table. I sat in the middle seat, separating her from the chair where Troy would sit. Since she was still afraid of Troy, I wanted her to see I could intercede and protect her if need be.

As we waited for Troy to arrive, her hazel eyes scrutinized everything in the room – vending machines, bookshelves, guard stations, children's play area, craft display cabinet – making sense of these as best she could. I prepared our table with books and cards and crayons and drawing paper.

She hid her emotion, smiling a beautiful white smile as Troy approached, like she was on a job interview.

Troy's yellow teeth smiled, but only slightly. He was obviously nervous. I hugged Troy, but before Hope had the chance to hug him, not that she would, he sat down, fidgeting.

She looked around searching for common ground to comment on, but found nothing. She brushed the bangs off her wrinkling forehead.

I opened the *Mother Goose* book in front of us.

"I hear you guys color and play cards?" Hope said.

"Sometimes," I said. "Huh, Troy?"

She lost herself in Troy's eyes, "What card game should we play?"

Troy nervously looked down, then to me for assistance.

"Uno or Rummy?" I asked.

Hope fingered the book, then said, "They have nice books here. Troy, do you read at all in here?" She was studying him intently, needing to decide for herself if he was for real or acting impaired.

Troy said, "Not much. Only when Thom is here."

She sounded chipper, "*Mother Goose*. She never goes out of style, does she?"

I started to speak, but felt my eyes welling with tears and my throat constricting, so I said nothing at all. Hope caught my eyes for a second, then quickly looked at the book.

Troy said, "Just go through and pick out a nursery rhyme, Hope. We can read it or play cards. Whatever you guys want to do."

She said, "Wow. Some real classics in here."

"HOPE"
(In the collection of Jill Bradley)

"The Old Woman Who Lived In The Shoe," I said. *"Old Mother Hub-bard."*

I remembered Mom reading that to me when I was a kid.

I thought about how glad Mom would be that the three of us were together. I remembered Rod's comment, stating: "When the mother goes, the family falls apart." Well, it wasn't true in our case. Through divorce, matricide, suicide, paranoia, and schizophrenia our family was still together. There were less of us, no doubt, but there were me and Hope and Troy.

Hope said, "Here's one that I remember Mom liked." Then reading, "What are little girls made of?"

Troy answered, "Sugar and Spice."

Hope read on, "Little girls are made of sugar and spice and everything nice. That's what little girls are made of. What are little boys made of?"

Troy said, "Snails."

Hope read on, "Snips and snails and puppy dog tails. That's what little boys are made of."

I said, "Sorry about that."

She smiled a genuine smile.

I added, "And Troy's sorry about that."

He nodded, looking frightened.

She almost burst into tears, but held them in. She looked completely destroyed, like she was seeing our mother's murdered body on the kitchen floor. I think all three of us saw that same image.

Then something came over Hope. Maybe it was the "mother" in her. Or maybe it was the "sister" in her. She composed herself and shuffled the cards, saying, "I like Rummy. I haven't played that in a very long time."

I nodded and said, "That sounds great. Let's play. You deal."

She spoke emotionally to Troy, "And I haven't played cards with you in so long. I think it's time we play cards. You're my brother after all."

Troy smiled, finally relaxing. He was forgiven now. As his eyes glazed, he handed me a choice of crayons and said, "Thom keeps score."

275

I chose the sepia-brown crayon, the color of Mom's eyes. I clutched it hard, then sat back in my chair as my sister's tiny hands dealt the cards.

In a minute, she and Troy sat back holding their cards – but they weren't looking at them. They were looking at each other.

They weren't smiling with their mouths, but their eyes smiled. I didn't know if they were seeing new people – or old, familiar ones.

I breathed in deep.

My fingers loosened around the sepia crayon and I put it down.

Thom's many visits with Troy from 1994-2009

___DREAM WORLD___

No pain   pleasure
No sorrow   Happiness
No lonlness   Friendship
No Distruction
No construction
No Death
LIFE

– TROY BIERDZ

Epilogue

W hen I return to Wisconsin, Hope sometimes joins me on visits with Troy; sometimes she doesn't. I try to honor her choices. I am grateful she summoned the courage for even one visit.

Like me, Hope is now against the death penalty; a major shift since many years ago, when Troy killed Mom, she wanted Troy put to death. She is also against a ban on gay marriage, indicating her acceptance and support of my sexuality.

• • •

Still, after almost eighteen years, I couldn't sleep for more than two hours in a row.

I'd always believed I could, or should, be able to take control of my anxiety and paranoia in public situations without the aid of drugs, excluding inhalers and alcohol of course. I also feared the damage an adverse reaction to a medication could cause. What if I ended up more nervous than I already was?

In 2007, with great trepidation, I finally visited several clinics and experimented with the various pills they prescribed for my anxiety and insomnia. Eventually, medication was found that could quiet the "noise" in my head, and let me sleep for at least four hours in a row at night. This extra two hours of sleep each night improved my life significantly. Oddly, I never questioned the benefits of medication to help Troy, only to treat myself.

Troy is amazingly healthy today. He is a model inmate. After a visit, I told a friend Troy was "one of the happiest people I know."

Our relationship is one of the most important in my life, but it is not completely resolved.

One night before I began using sleeping pills, I was woken by a loud crash in my bedroom. Half asleep and fully afraid, I jumped blindly out of bed and thought I was being attacked. I tried to scream, "No, Troy!" Like in a nightmare, no sound came out of my mouth. I woke up pointing toward the window, screaming, "No! No! No!"

In my stupor, I believed Troy had broken in my window and was finally going to kill me. The crash was caused by a painting falling off the wall.

Forgiving Troy is not something I can do just once; I must do it every day.

People ask me, "Could your mother's murder have been prevented? Could something have been done to save her – to save them?"

I don't know if they could have been saved. All I know for certain is to experience true freedom, whether your prison bars are real or self-imposed by your own mind, you must learn to forgive.

That's the last thing Mom asked me to do.

Painting at Katrina fundraiser   Scarlett Johansson at Soicher-Marin
hosted by Kathie Griffin

The Art

In 2004, I met Joe Argazzi in a spiritual study group and we quickly became friends. He deeply believes in the message of my story to help others heal and has been unwavering in his support. As he learned of my passion for painting and the ease I felt in front of a canvas, he asked to look at my work. Seeing the hundreds of paintings, he encouraged me to pursue a career in art. Joe was responsible for my red-carpet art premier hosted by actress Scarlett Johansson at The Sochier Marin Gallery in Los Angeles. This spectacular night was also a fundraising event for The Art of Elysium children's charity. The show displayed twenty walls of my paintings; two-hundred-and-fifty of my works in expressionism, impressionism, surrealism, and symbolism. I am both grateful and humbled to say that as of this writing, my art has raised more than $100,000 for charities.

Thom recieves Thalian's Key To The Light award
from Debbie Reynolds and Ruta Lee

Painting at Connie Stevens' charity

Painting at charity hosted by
Rosalyn Carter

It was the beginning of a new career for me that I am
absolutely passionate about.

In 2005, I received the VOX/Out Emerging Voices of Style +
Design Award. In 2006 I started to receive invitations to go
around the country to create a painting "live" during charity
events. The finished art would then be auctioned off to the
highest bidder. I found this to be very successful both in
raising money and awareness for organizations I believe in.
Flying to different cities to paint live brought back memories
of my soap opera mall appearances. But this was different.
This time I didn't have to pretend to be someone else. This
time I could relax, be myself and do something I love to
do.The following years brought art shows across the
country, as well as a floating exhibit on a transatlantic voyage
on the Queen Mary 2.

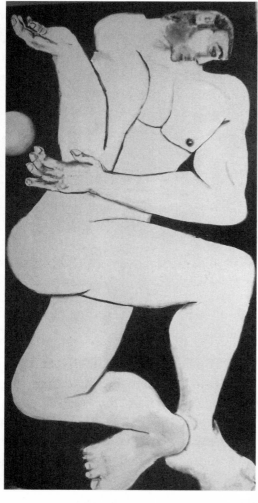

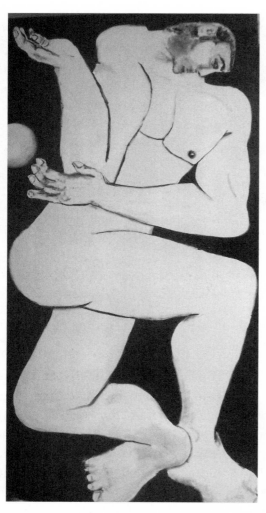

Art Biography by Joe Argazzi

"What emerges from his personal journey onto the canvas is at times heartbreaking, haunting and profoundly affecting. His body of work ultimately proves to be an uplifting and inspiring experience of transcendence, a compelling testimony on the resilience of the human spirit. Thom's need to express his inner feelings on canvas became an obsession. "Each painting became an earnest attempt to make sense out of the senseless; to make something beautiful out of something tragic."

"Contradictory strategies for painting has quickly become Bierdz hallmark. Although he uses the same touch throughout, it can at times appear to be a number of different voices, even personalities. The reluctance to lay claim to a fixed position might at one time have been attributed to youth but it is clearly now an integral aspect of his methodology. Nothing

is by chance. Even when the form appears to be a sort of free association, that's really his expertise in terms of handling paint. The process is at times extremely rigorous and other times purely subconscious.

In the end, Thom allows the work to speak for itself. The very thing that takes our breath away, his vulnerability, his strength and sensitivities are the same roads we all walk. He holds a sort of universal mirror, encouraging us to look at ourselves, and with a bold conviction and honesty, embrace all of who we are."

Please go to www.ThomBierdz.com
for prison footage of Thom visiting Troy in
1995, and to see hundreds of paintings in color
including the paintings in this book.

Visit Thom's website blog to follow his
recent career accomplishments. Read interviews
on Thom's coming full-circle, 20 years later,
to play Phillip Chancellor III again on
The Young and the Restless.